GOING
YARD

GOING YARD

The Ultimate Guide For Major League Baseball Stadium Road Trips

STAN FRIDSTEIN

WITH MORE THAN A BIT OF HELP FROM

ERIC FRIDSTEIN

My lawyer told me to write this

This book is written as a source of information. Every effort has been made to ensure the accuracy of the information as of the publication date. The author visited each MLB website to update pricing, hours of operation, tour information, URL addresses, services offered and the like. He went through the same process with substantially every activity described herein. However, things change all the time and the author disclaims responsibility for any adverse effects directly or indirectly arising out of the use of information contained herein.

Dedication

This book is dedicated to three people: My wife Gail, for her selfless nature and overwhelming desire to create strong bonds across our family; my daughter Allie, whose spirit, humor, intellectual curiosity and serious lack of jealousy associated with her brother's baseball trips astound me to no end; and my son Eric, who is an inspiration to me every day and provided the best travel partner anyone could ever ask for as we journeyed together across 19 states (and Canada) to visit the 30 Major League Baseball parks. I am blessed to have the three of them in my life.

Contents

Preface

"There are 30…"

"I'm pretty sure there are 32."

"Dad, I'm telling you, there are 30 major league baseball parks. You're thinking of the NFL, where there are 32 teams. In baseball, there are only 30 teams between the two leagues."

A quick trip to mlb.com certified Eric Fridstein's superior understanding of everything that is baseball. This wouldn't be embarrassing to me were in not for the fact that Eric was only 8 years old at the time.

This conversation took place at the home of Kelvin, Carolyn, Ryan and Sara Yamashita.

As our baseball dialog progressed, it began to blossom into something seemingly larger than life. Kelvin looked at me and asked, "What do you think about taking the boys to visit every single major league ballpark over the next few years?"

It was an interesting proposition. It would involve taking a less than full family trip every single summer for a number of years with a couple of young boys. There would be planes, trains and automobiles. There would be scheduling and logistical nightmares. There was the potential for outrageous expenses, given the costs of airfare, hotels, ballgame tickets, food, and car rentals.

What would we do with the boys during the off hours? Games are generally about 3 hours long...what forms of entertainment would fill the other 21 hours each day? These were high energy, less than perfectly focused eight year olds.

How would we get around? When would we fly? When would we drive? How would we keep the boys from falling into insufferable boredom during the long road trips between cities? Where would we stay? Would it be better to be near the ballparks, the airports, the city centers or in the safest part of each town?

How would we make the games interesting? Let's face it; 8 year old boys, each with the attention span of a gnat, could make things challenging. If we were going to visit all 30 ballparks, we were clearly signing up for some boring games played by teams in which we have no interest. What could we do to spice things up even during the worst of games? How could we make every game special and memorable?

So many questions popped up. There were no easy answers. And there were no known resources available to us. Nevertheless, we persevered and decided to give it a try the following baseball season.

We would call the summer of 2004 our test year. We'd pick a region with a handful of teams, try to find a week to ten day period in which they were all in town and just plain figure things out. The legwork would be very inefficient, since we were going through the planning process for the first time. Frankly, we didn't even know if it would work. Our goal was simple enough: To create a favorable enough experience that would make us enthusiastic about moving forward in 2005. And 2006. And beyond.

We agreed upfront this endeavor was all about the journey and not about the destinations. While visiting 30 stadiums was a presumptuous and maybe preposterous goal, we knew the memories created along the way would be the real reward. The more cities and stadiums, the more memories.

One critically important comment must be noted at this point in time: We knew the entire ordeal would be derailed before it left the station if our spouses weren't onboard with the program. As with most healthy households, Kelvin and I were keenly aware of our subordinated household positions in the decision-tree. As such, spousal support was crucial since these trips would entail considerable financial obligations, family vacation compromises and other issues that needed to be fully discussed prior to taking this nonsense too far.

Fortunately, we had the foresight to have married women who fully supported this folly. They liked the idea of creating an additional reason for father-son bonding experiences and felt it would craft a lifetime of memories for everyone. With their full support, we forged ahead with reckless abandon.

As we began researching the process of putting our first trip together, we asked our baseball-nut friends if they knew others who had successfully completed the journey upon which we were about to embark. While almost everyone with whom we spoke thought it was an exciting idea, there were no known experts on the subject. We were unable to locate any books or find any descriptions online that provided a comprehensive look at this journey. There were books about ballparks. But there wasn't a go-to source for helping to craft entire trips centered on ballparks that also covered the plethora of other activities available to us.

It became clearer and clearer that we were the Lewis and Clark of Major League Baseball Park visits. Others had traveled the path but none had mapped it out in easy-to-follow terms.

We promised ourselves that if The Fearless Foursome (as we called ourselves) successfully made it to every stadium, we'd let others know how best to plan their own journeys. We'd give them helpful hints, tips, places to visit in each MLB town, travel plans, and so much more.

While each and every trip would be unique and special, some basic underlying direction would surely help enhance the experience. At a minimum, our guide would make the process of planning these adventures far easier for others.

Our hope and desire is that this book inspires others to visit numerous if not every Major League Ballpark; to create experiences and memories that would last forever, to see things in cities they would never otherwise visit, to meet people from other parts of the country and understand and embrace the specialness of the natural cultural differences, to experience regional food preferences, to gain perspective on the overwhelming size of this great nation, and to witness history from a point of view not offered in textbooks (our boys stood in Dealy Plaza on the actual spot where John F. Kennedy was assassinated, touched the car in which he rode at the Henry Ford Museum in Detroit and visited his gravesite at Arlington National Cemetery).

Then there were those wonderful nights after each game when we'd return to our hotel rooms, shut off the lights and relive the game, the stadium and the day. It was oftentimes in those quiet moments that we had our deepest, most meaningful conversations about something even more important than baseball: Life. We'd talk about everything. We'd discuss all the stuff we couldn't delve into when others were around. We'd share secrets because our mutual defense mechanisms were down. We weren't father and son. We were a couple of close friends spending the best moments of our lives together. It was magic. And I'm not sure it can ever be replicated.

In retrospect, that's what these trips were really all about. The ballparks are special because each is unique and many are loaded with history. But in the end, the stadiums were nothing more than a foil for something much larger. This was the greatest father-son bonding experience of our lives. We treasure the seven year run and experiences we shared and will selfishly hold onto them all the way to our graves.

So here it is: A how-to guide for visiting every Major League Baseball Park and all that goes with it. I can only hope your journey is as enjoyable and fulfilling as ours. Enjoy the ride. It's a great one.

Chapter 1: Some Planning Tips

The first thing you need to decide is how many years you're willing to invest in this journey. Here are a few questions you'll want to address:

- ❖ What is your annual budget?

- ❖ Are you going exclusively with your child(ren) or are you adding another family or friend to the mix?

- ❖ How much time are you able to allocate each year?

- ❖ How old are the travelers?

Setting up a budget

"Due to budgetary overruns, the light at the end of the tunnel has been turned off."

> *— Anonymous*

Here's the deal with money: You'll spend less money in total by condensing the number of trips and visiting more parks per trip. You'll need fewer cross country flights and car rental rates will be less per day. The flip side of this financial equation, however, means you'll spend more money per trip each year. As a result, you need to think long and hard about how much you can comfortably afford to spend and how many years you have available for these trips. Here are categories of expenses (and a few cost savings tips) you're likely face as you prepare your budget:

Airfare	Book flights well in advance and look for deals
Airport parking	If you can get a spouse to drop you at the airport, you'll save some money.
Car Rentals/Gas	In some markets, you can use public transportation. Do this when possible. Not only will you save money on parking, gas and the car rental fee, but you won't have to race to the car rental return facility at the airport when you bolt to the next town. Don't get a small car for gas saving purposes. At the risk of upsetting the "Greenies", you'll need a lot of trunk space for the suitcases. What's more, a small car gets awfully claustrophobic in the back seat making those long driving trips even longer.
Game Tickets	There's an entire section in this guide that describes how best to secure free or very cheap tickets. However, ticket prices can be very inexpensive in the bleachers or very costly in the VIP sections. Your budget tolerance will dictate your seating location at each ballpark.
Ballpark Food	It's a rip-off. Let's face it, once you're in the ballpark, you're a captive audience and management knows it. There are two schools of thought here: The value shopper eats before or after the game outside the stadium.

	The purist wants the entire ballpark experience, and food is part of the deal. Come on…can you really absorb the full baseball game experience without a hot dog and some peanuts? We didn't think so.
Other Food	Man cannot live on ballpark food alone. You'll need to budget for non-ballpark meals on the road. Some cities are extremely expensive (like New York) and others are super cheap. One helpful hint, try to book hotels that include breakfast…that's one less meal to pay for each day.
Other Activities	While the boys are convinced that we went on baseball trips, the dads were wise enough to know we were taking in cities that included trips to the ballpark. MLB cities are typically large, culturally interesting, historically meaningful and very cool places. Each city has plethora of things to do and see. You'll want to wallet for as many activities in each city as your budget and schedule can afford. Some of your best memories will not take place in the ballparks. Later in this guide, I have pointed out highlights in each market. We would encourage you to take advantage of the sights as you may never return to many of these cities.
Hotels	We stayed at inexpensive, safe, clean hotels. Some were near the ballparks and others near the airport or city center. We elected to spend our money on things more important to us than expensive lodging. Hampton Inn, Marriott Courtyard and other similar hotel chains offer a good environment, clean rooms, frequently have pools and generally include breakfast for a nominal extra fee.
Other	There will be other costs such as mass transportation in the larger cities, ballpark parking, gift shops and the like that need to be included in your budget.

As you can imagine, the budget for your trip can vary dramatically based on any number of variables.

Below is a simple budget calculator to help you with your cost estimates. We've included some very rough assumptions to provide general guidance. The estimates below assume the following:

◈ Your group will fly into one MLB market, rent a car, drive to all cities in the region and then return the car at the airport at the final destination before flying home.

◈ You'll be traveling with another family.

◈ Your group will visit 5 ballparks in five different cities on each trip.

◈ Your group includes a set of 2 adults and 2 kids. Car rental and gas charges will be evenly split between the families.

◈ Each adult/child will share a hotel room. If you want to shoehorn all four of you into a single room, take 40% off the hotel estimate.

◈ You will be gone for a total of 7 days and 7 nights.

◈ You will find activities during non-game hours in each city.

Cost Estimator

Item	Assumption	Estimated Cost per Family
Airfare/Parking	We averaged about $400 per person in airfare and $4 per day per person for parking at the airport.	$850
Car Rental/Gas	Figure about $60 per day for the car rental and $12 per day for gas. This is a shared cost between the two groups.	$250
Game Tickets	Assume an average of $45 per ticket per game. We'll give you some tips for acquiring the occasional free set of seats later in the book.	$450
Ballpark Food	About $25 per person per game and this assumes you have the ability to say "no" to the vendors marching up and down the aisles selling popcorn, peanuts, licorice, cotton candy and other essentials.	$250
Other Food	Free breakfasts at hotel most of the time and a non-ballpark meal each day. You'll also need to score some munchies or water along the way. $75 per family per day is a good starting point.	$525
Activities	Some are free and others will cost. Figure $50 per day per family.	$350
Hotels	Varies widely, but we averaged $125 per day per room.	$875
Other	These costs will come up and there's no way to avoid them. Figure $50 per day per family.	$350
Total		**$3,900**

The budget outlined above is fully loaded. Some of the trips will not require airfare. Others may present the opportunity to touch base with old friends (a euphemism for camping out at their homes at no charge). Many of the best urban activities are absolutely free (such as walking around the Mall in Washington DC, cruising Central Park in New York City, and poking around the Lincoln Park Zoo in Chicago). If you focus on these sorts of activities, you'll bring your expenses down considerably.

Once you begin planning your trip, just use the calculator above and you'll have a better handle on the projected costs of your custom designed trip.

Do it alone or invite another family?
That is the question...

"The real voyage of discovery consists not in seeking new land-scapes but in having new eyes."

— Marcel Proust

Selecting your traveling companion(s) is perhaps biggest the decision you'll have to make. For us, the choice was easy. We hatched the idea together and evolved it into a plan as a team. Both fathers and sons were already close friends and had previous travel experience together, so compatibility was never an issue.

There are clear advantages of taking on this adventure with an additional family. As discussed earlier, there are some cost advantages, however they turned out to be rather minor compared to the other, less obvious benefits.

When it came to planning the trip, we grossly underestimated the amount of preparation time required. If either of us had to take on the full responsibility of figuring out which section of the country we were going to carve out each year, matching up every team's schedule against the others in their region, discovering and implementing the best ways of securing game tickets, handling hotel and car rental research, purchasing airline tickets, determining activities in each and every city as they revolve around game time schedules and, well, you get the idea...it would have been pretty overwhelming.

We split up the duties in a way that made the job less daunting for each of us. This is how it worked for us:

Stan

◈ Split the country into regions (more about this later) and overlay each team's home schedule for the entire summer.

◈ Find the week (or so) that every team in a region would be playing at home.

◈ Identify and implement creative ways of securing tickets and ballpark experiences for each ballgame.

Kelvin

◈ Research the best travel options (air, train, car, mass transportation) for each trip.

◈ Purchase all airline tickets and car rentals.

◈ Determine the best hotel options in each market and make reservations.

Both

◈ Research and recommend great activities in each city visited.

It was a lot of work each year and we were thankful for the help provided by the corresponding partner. Splitting the duties worked quite well because of a mutual willingness to regularly communicate.

In addition, we had to be sensitive to certain personal preferences, budget constraints, scheduling conflicts and other issues that might get in the way of a great trip. We talked all the time about our ideas, the status of our efforts and instances in which we could use a hand. It worked extremely well and candidly, neither of us would have wanted to take on the entire load alone. In addition, by creating an ongoing dialog about the progress of our work, we built an air of excitement around each trip that piqued as the departure date approached.

An additional reason to consider going with another family is the need for the boys to be boys. Hey, each of our sons loves the company of his father. But 24/7 is a bit tough even in the best of circumstances. Sometimes, boys just want to jump up and down on their beds, play Marco Polo in a swimming pool, and hang with a buddy. What's more, those long drives between cities (did you know it's over 6 hours between Kansas City and Minneapolis!?) are a lot shorter when the boys are busy playing video games, telling silly jokes or sharing a conversation in the back seat of the car.

The first step in choosing your partners on this journey is to make sure everyone is compatible. While this seems obvious, you need to understand that if one person grates on the others, the trips will be miserable. What's more, if each family has a different definition of the term "reasonable budget", things can get very strained. For example, we made the decision to spend more money on baseball park tickets and in-city experiences and make a tradeoff by staying at less expensive hotels. If one of us was a Four Seasons type of person and wouldn't be happy unless the ballpark seats were located in VIP sections, it would have strained our relationship considerably. These issues are important to discuss upfront.

If your group hasn't traveled together before, it isn't a bad idea to take a mini-trip together (it may or may not include baseball) to see how well everyone gets along before starting your baseball park journey. Many people get together socially for a few hours every few weeks but can't be with one another 24/7 (and you *will* be together constantly during these trips!). It's better to surface any key issues prior to making a commitment of this magnitude.

Telling the boys upfront that you plan to visit every MLB ballpark may set them up for serious disappointment if you decide to discontinue your effort earlier than expected. And if you don't go forward, you will be going back on your word and that has its own set of implications. Here is our recommendation: Rather than telling the boys you plan to visit every MLB park upfront, tell them you'd like to visit a bunch of really cool stadiums in a different section of the country the following summer and leave it at that. At the end of the trip, if you all feel positive about the experience, offer it up for the next season. Before you know it, this will become an annual event and you'll be well on your way to visiting each and every ballpark. It's a subtle approach, but one that could very well pay dividends if things don't work out as planned.

Here is something of critical importance: Everyone involved must be quite passionate about baseball. It sounds obvious, but we know of other fathers who love baseball and think a trip like this might inspire that passion within their child. It doesn't work that way. You're going to see baseball, talk baseball and live baseball for an extended term each summer for many years. Everyone involved must have a real love of the game. Let's face it, most ballgame games will pit two teams against one another for which you have no serious preference. Many games will not be exciting. Some stadiums aren't very special. There will be days when the weather isn't cooperative. Star players frequently sit out games. Several stadiums are not particularly fan friendly. You may get stuck in some crummy seat locations. All of these obstacles and others can be easily overcome if there is a genuine affection for the game. Without real fervor, many games will become a drag and the overall experience will be less than positive.

How much time to allocate each year

"Events in our lives happen in a sequence in time, but in their significance to us they find their own order."

– Eudora Welty

There are several factors that will ultimately determine how many years it takes to complete your journey. Some are within your control and others are not.

Financial resources will play an important role in the consideration set. Most families have some sort of annual travel budget. This trip will most likely be one of several vacations taken each year. As a result, you'll probably want to set a budget upfront (see the Cost Estimator on Page 5).

There are a few things you can do to help reduce costs in certain years if you know upfront you will be on a tighter budget. One way to accomplish this is to see local/drivable stadiums in a year when money is tighter (or an expensive family trip is already on the drawing board). Another way to save in those budget-challenged years is to plan trips in cities in which you have free places to stay (friends and relatives). However, let's be clear: If you are planning to hit all 30 stadiums over the course of time, you're going to need to think about the overall cost commitment before you start. And it won't be insignificant.

Sometimes, the number of stadiums you visit per season will be limited by the Scheduling Gods. You're going to break the country into a number of geographic regions and begin charting out your course of action each year. There may be instances when the teams in the region you'd like to visit are simply not in town the same 7-10 day period during the entire season. It happens. In fact, it is somewhat intentional. Major League Baseball scheduling planners make every effort to limit the number of home games played at the same time by competing teams within a city. They don't want the Cubs and White Sox in Chicago at the same time. Ditto the Giants and Athletics in the Bay Area. Ditto again the Yankees and Mets in New York, and, to a lesser degree, the Nationals and Orioles in Washington/Baltimore. This can play havoc with your scheduling and may cause you to have to re-visit certain sections of the country.

Here's another thing to think about at the genesis of your planning process: You may have to consider how pure you want to be when making the following statement: "We've visited every single MLB stadium." Since your journey will probably take many years to complete, new stadiums will undoubtedly be built during the transom. You may or may not want to return to these cities at some point in order to stay current. As of this writing, five stadiums have been built since our initial visits: Yankees, Mets, Nationals, Twins and Cardinals. And there's more than a bit of discussion about the Florida Marlins moving into a new home. What's more, there are constant rumors about franchises moving to new markets and the occasional discussion of a new expansion team. We haven't decided how best to approach this issue…your decision will be a personal one, too. However, it's safe to assume that between scheduling conflicts, new stadiums and possible rainouts (yes, there is the chance of an occasional rainout), the journey may well take longer than initially planned. Be sure to factor that into your preparation process.

By the way, almost all stadiums have been rebuilt in the last 15 years. Here's an interesting fact: Dodger Stadium is the third oldest in major league baseball (after Fenway and Wrigley). It's pretty amazing that an entire transformation from old school stadiums has yielded so many very cool, often retro-designed ballparks with loads of accoutrements in such a short period of time. There are really only two or three teams remaining that are even remotely interested in building new stadiums in the next 5 to 10 years: Florida, Tampa Bay and Oakland. You may want to keep this in mind as you plan your trips and place these teams at the end of your journey, if possible.

Another consideration relative to how many stadiums you want to visit each year has to do with the age and traveling capacity of the participants. Generally speaking, there is an inverse relationship between the age of a child and the difficulties presented by extended and often complicated travel. There will be many instances when you will be waking up at the crack of dawn to hit the road or catch a flight to the next city. You will arrive at game time, head to the hotel afterward and repeat this activity the next day. And the next day. And the day after that. It can be very challenging for young kids living out of suitcases to make the adjustment. You'll want to be sensitive to this issue as you plan your trip each year. As a general guideline, our boys were eight years old when we began visiting out of town ballparks. They were terrific. However, we wouldn't recommend taking kids any younger too far or for too long.

Then there's the issue of homesickness. You'll have to make the call on this one. Our boys had no such issues, but we've spoken to other fathers whose sons were miserable on the road and crying for their mother mid-way through the trip. You (or more specifically, your wife) will be the best judge of trip length. As a general guideline, the younger the child, the shorter the trip.

At the other end of the age spectrum will be kids who may either lose interest or be unavailable to complete the journey due to age. For example, if your child is in college, he may only have a few years until he becomes a full time member of the work force. Once there, his scheduling flexibility and vacation time may be handicapped to the point of making a complete stadium tour impossible. While this isn't the end of the world, it's something to consider if you're a goal-oriented person and you've set the bar at reaching all thirty ballparks. In this case, you'll want to consider visiting more parks per year and even using the occasional weekend to hit a few parks located closer to home.

Scheduling Strategy

"It pays to plan ahead. It wasn't raining when Noah built the ark."

–Anonymous

If you weren't sleeping through your grade school U.S. Geography class, you'll probably recall that the United States is a big place. In fact, it's really big and seems to be larger still when you find yourself driving across much of its great expanse.

That's why you'll want to plan your trips by breaking the United States into smaller, more approachable regions. By doing this, you'll get a much better handle on how many ballparks you'll want to visit each year and you'll also be setting the table for the beginning of some scheduling research.

As we studied the location of each ballpark, we broke the ballpark geography down into manageable pieces:

The West Coast (7 teams):

Los Angeles (Dodgers and Angels)
The Bay Area (Giants and Athletics)
Seattle
San Diego
Arizona

Midwest (6 teams):

Chicago (Cubs and White Sox)
Milwaukee
St. Louis
Kansas City
Minneapolis

Mideast (5 teams):

Toronto
Detroit
Cleveland
Pittsburgh
Cincinnati

East Coast (6 teams)

Washington DC
Baltimore
Philadelphia
New York (Mets and Yankees)
Boston

South (5 teams)

Houston
Dallas
Atlanta
Miami
Tampa Bay

Mountain (1 team)

Colorado

The next step is to create a spreadsheet that breaks the country into the regional buckets described above. Along the top of the spreadsheet, make room for the dates in which your group is available (we typically started with the first day of summer vacation and finished with the last day of summer vacation). You'll want to be sure to black out any periods that are unavailable, such as already planned family events or trips, summer school or other obligations.

The sample spreadsheet above only shows the month of June, but it typifies how this method begins to make it apparent which section of the country will be most viable in any given year.

Now it's time to take out a map to determine which region offers the least amount of driving. More specifically, you don't want to backtrack if you can avoid it (for example, you wouldn't want to see the Chicago Cubs, drive to Kansas City for a Royals game and then head back to Chicago to catch the White Sox). Here's a quick way to determine the approximate mileage between each city: Go to http://www.symsys.com/~ingram/mileage/index.php and use their Mileage Calculator. Funny how you find these nifty little tools, huh? I have no idea how these guys make money on this mileage calculator. They probably make less on their website than I'll make on this book. And that's pitiful. However, I digress…

Sample Scheduling Grid (from our 2005 Trip)

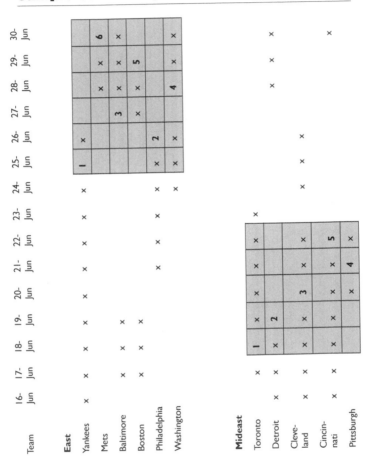

Using the Sample Scheduling Grid example above, we ruled out the East Coast in favor of the Mideast ballparks this particular year because the Mideast home-stands provided the opportunity to travel from park to park in the same direction, thus minimizing time on the road and optimizing the time spent in cities doing interesting activities. As a result, we flew into Toronto, caught a train to Detroit and traveled by car to Cleveland, Pittsburgh and Cincinnati. What made this itinerary ideal was the need to drive through Canton, Ohio on the leg from Pittsburgh to Cincinnati. Canton houses the National Football League Hall of Fame, and we didn't want to miss that for the world (and you won't either!).

Major League Baseball typically releases the upcoming season's schedule around New Year's. Go to Major League Baseball's schedule planner: http://mlb.mlb.com/mlb/schedule/team_by_team.jsp. You'll see every team listed on this page. Click on a team's sortable schedule and direct it to list only home games. It'll list every single home game by month. This will become an invaluable research tool for you.

Once you've set up your spreadsheet, you can place an "x" in the appropriate date box for each team by region during the date range you've defined for your trip (see the Sample Schedule on the last page for reference). When you've completed the regions, it's relatively easy to spot the 7-10 day period that finds all the teams in each region playing home-stands. Then you simply use a map to ensure you have selected the schedule offering the most efficient drives.

Your first season will offer many opportunities since you'll have so many options available to you. As the years go by and you begin to complete various regions, your searches will be limited to the few remaining regions left to visit. As you can imagine, your options will diminish substantially. By way of example, our next to last set of parks included Northern California (Giants and A's) and Seattle. In 2009, there was only one three-day period during the entire baseball season that found all three teams in town at the same time. Had we not been available to go that weekend (we were generously given hall passes for Memorial Day weekend by our spouses), it would have required two trips and the associated incremental costs.

Here's an important tip: You'll be visiting 26 different major markets as you journey to all the ballparks. Unless you and your child are far better traveled than most, many ballparks are located in cities you've never been to and will otherwise have no reason to visit in the future. Every single market that houses an MLB team is relatively large and has some interesting things to see. Some cities are downright amazing in that they attract travelers the world over. If you're planning to spend the time and money to get there, you should make every effort to invest a bit more on the special things to see and do. We cannot possibly overstate the importance of this advice to you. Many of our best memories have nothing to do with the ballparks or ballgames.

We're going to give you very specific ideas about what to do in each market later in the book, but suffice it to say that extending a 7 day trip to 9 or 10 days to make time for sightseeing will be well worth it, schedules providing. Our sons' perspective of the country and each city has tremendous texture as a result of these trips and those memories can't be recreated in a lifetime of travels. Don't think exclusively about ballparks. Think city experiences.

Planes, trains or automobiles?

"Never travel with more children than you have car windows."
—Erma Bombeck

Hopefully this guide is being read by people from all parts of the country and beyond. As a result, the need to fly to different regions for baseball games will be somewhat dependent upon the location of your home base. Nevertheless, flying will undoubtedly be part of your transportation solution at some point of this journey.

A few tips about flying. First, look for deals. This may seem obvious, but most of the airlines jack up their prices during the busy summer months (it's called yield pricing...the fuller the plane, the more expensive the tickets. And they tend to be fuller during the summer vacation months.).

Since you will probably be locking into your summer baseball schedule in January each year, there's no reason to hold off making your airline reservations.

When you make your reservations, if at all possible, go for non-stop flights. There are a couple of reasons (beyond the obvious ones) that make non-stops worth the extra money. First of all, you'll be packing a fair amount of clothing (you'll be gone for a week on average and won't want to spend time laundering clothing on the road) and this may require you to check your luggage. The more stops your flight makes, the greater the chances of losing a bag. A lost suitcase on this kind of trip is a real nightmare since you'll be in a different city almost every day, making it almost impossible for the airline to remarry you to your lost luggage on a timely basis.

Another reason to pursue non-stop flights is that you will generally fly into a market on game day. If you miss your connection for some reason you'll risk missing the game. It's challenging enough to weave the labyrinth of options together in order to create a schedule; you certainly wouldn't want to blow up your plans because of a missed connection.

When you book your flights, be sure to book each person's ticket at the same time. While this creates some accounting issues between the families (not a big deal), you need to make sure you're all on the same flight. The logistical nightmares created by juggling multiple flight schedules are headaches you want to avoid.

When should you drive and when should you fly? Our general rule of thumb: If the drive is over 6 hours, we'd recommend that you fly. More than six hours on the road will leave the average kid pretty cranky. What's more, it's time that could otherwise be spent checking out a city's highlights. As mentioned earlier in this guide, there is a good chance you won't return to many of the cities visited during your lifetime. It would be a pity to miss a city's attractions because you spent an extra few hours on the road.

One of our more exciting excursions was the trip from Toronto to Detroit. Here's a bit of travel trivia you may find enlightening: You can't rent a car in Canada and return it in the United States (at least not if you use any of the major car rental companies). Rather than flying between the two cities, we purchased Via Rail Canada tickets and caught a nice glimpse of the Canadian countryside in the comfort of our speeding train. At four and a half hours, it was undoubtedly faster than dealing with an international flight (Toronto to Detroit) and a whole lot more fun. Oh, and the tickets were probably half the price. For more information, go to: http://www.viarail.ca.

Where should you stay?

"We need inn-experienced people."
                                    —Actual sign outside a hotel

If you are looking to save money and reconnect with old friends, you may want to consider staying at their homes while on the road.

We felt the need to be strategically located in each city and within arm's length of the sights outweighed the financial benefits offered up by staying at the homes of our friends. Only once did we stay at a buddy's home (and we thank him at the end of the book in the Acknowledgments section).

So where should you stay on your trip? The answer is dependent upon your schedule, the city, the stadium's location and your dependence on mass transportation.

Let's start with your schedule. If you have an early flight out of town following a night game, you'll probably want to stay near the airport. That way, you can return the car following a night game (or an evening's activities after a day game) and simply take the shuttle to the airport in the morning.

If you plan to eschew a car rental for mass transportation in a particular city, be sure to book a hotel close to a major departure point (train or subway stop). You don't want to be dragging your luggage halfway across the city to your hotel.

Some cities have exciting inner city activities and you'll want to be part of the action. Cities such as Chicago, San Francisco, New York and Boston have plethora of things to do in their respective city centers. It would be a pity to miss out on all the action by staying merely within striking distance. The cities mentioned above also have fine mass transportation, providing easy access to their respective ballparks from the city center.

Where to stay by market and stadium

City/Stadium	Where to Stay
Chicago/Wrigley Field	City Center or Near Stadium
Chicago/US Cellular Field	City Center
Milwaukee/Miller Park	City Center
St. Louis/Busch	Near Stadium
Kansas City/Kauffman Stadium	City Center
Minneapolis/Target Field	City Center is Near Stadium
Toronto/Rogers Centre	City Center is Near Stadium
Detroit/Comerica Park	City Center
Cleveland/Progressive Park	Near Stadium
Pittsburgh/PNC Park	Near Stadium
Cincinnati/Great American Ballpark	Near Stadium
Washington DC/Nationals Stadium	City Center
Baltimore/Camden Yards	Inner Harbor Near Stadium
Philadelphia/Citizens Bank Park	City Center
New York/Yankees Stadium	City Center
New York/Citi Field	City Center
Boston/Fenway Park	Near Stadium
Houston/Minute Maid Park	City Center
Dallas/The Ballpark at Arlington	City Center or Near Stadium
Atlanta/Turner Field	City Center, ideally Buckhead
Miami/Marlins Park	Miami Beach or South Beach
Tampa Bay/Tropicana Field	City Center in St. Petersburg
Denver/Coors Field	City Center
Phoenix/Chase Field	City Center or Scottsdale
San Francisco/AT&T Park	City Center is Near Stadium
Oakland/Coliseum	San Francisco City Center
Los Angeles/Dodger Stadium	City Center, Beverly Hills, Santa Monica
Anaheim/Angel Stadium	Anaheim near Disneyland, or see LA
San Diego/Petco Park	Near Stadium

In some cases, the ballparks are located in a great part of town. In such instances, it's ideal to stay by the ballpark. It's a completely different experience when you can walk to and from the stadium and feel the energy of the crowd. It's also nice to avoid exiting crowded parking lots or waiting in line for trains and/or subways. What's more, most of the time, visiting teams stay in hotels near the ballparks, so there's a fair chance you'll score an opportunity to meet some players along the way. Unfortunately, not all stadiums are located in a desirable part of town and you certainly don't want to feel unsafe with your surroundings.

All issues described on the previous page aside, here is a chart that outlines the cities where you'll want to stay by the ballpark, if you can.

Chapter 2: Some Basic Ground Rules

How to keep the games interesting

"I'm astounded by people who want to know the universe when it's hard enough to find your way around Chinatown."

—Woody Allen

The most important goal of these trips is to have fun.

While this would appear to be a rather obvious statement, in practice it can be a bit challenging. To visit every stadium means you'll be seeing every team. Let's face it, some teams aren't very good. They don't have an exciting roster and they may not be playing well. And as often as not, these ho-hum teams will be playing similarly ho-hum teams. To make matters worse, even if one or both teams playing on a particular day is a good team, you may find yourself in a less than exciting game. And the star players are rested from time to time, which can make a game a bit less exciting to watch.

More specifically, we visited 30 ballparks and caught only three game-winning hits (Cubs, Red Sox and Nationals). Most of the games weren't exactly fingernail biters. Some were blowouts that resulted in a clearing of the stands by the seventh inning stretch. If you don't believe us, go to the sports section of your newspaper on any given day during the baseball season and look at the scores. Most of the games were decided by more than 2 runs.

So the question becomes: How do you keep every game interesting? How do you make for a great ballpark experience when some parks aren't much fun? How do you ensure that everyone involved has a good time at every single game?

Out solution: We created games within each game.

We created one game called Count the Bases. Here's how it works. There are two sides (in our case, we had the dads pitted against the sons). The dads and sons drafted players from the two teams playing on that particular day. Each father or son side selected 3 players from each of the baseball teams along with a few alternates in case a selected player took the day off.

To start the process, you'll want to flip a coin and the winner of the coin toss may elect to either secure the first draft pick or defer and take the next two. After that, each team picks one selection until the rosters are filled.

To make things clear, the boys' and dads' rosters will each have 3 players for both teams on the field that day. They will also each have 2 alternates from each team on their roster.

The goal of the game is draft the roster that generates the most total bases. You keep track of every single base accumulated by the players on each side (boys versus dads). The team with the most total bases at the conclusion of the game wins. A word of warning: If your kid plays Nintendo baseball, he or she will have a decided advantage. Nintendo provides all sorts of statistical data not readily available to the average fan. Information such as batting averages at night versus day games, how a batter fares against right handed versus left handed pitchers, and other meaningful tidbits are common knowledge to regular Nintendo MLB players. Forewarned is forearmed.

Here is what a typical Drafting Form looks like (there is a full page version of this Drafting Form in the back of the book and it's yours to photocopy):

Game date:

Teams: _____ vs _____

Home Team:

Boys: Dads:

_____   _____

_____   _____

_____   _____

Visiting Team:

Boys: Dads:

_____   _____

_____   _____

_____   _____

Alternates:

Boys: Dads:

_____   _____

_____   _____

<u>**Total Bases**</u>

Boys: Dads:

Each base safely reached by a drafted player gets credited to either the boys' or dads' team. It doesn't matter how a player reaches base or progresses to the next (hit, walk, steal, hit by pitcher, error, fielder's choice, advanced by hit, etc.). Have the kids keep score when possible as it makes the game more interesting for them. Even the most boring games were fun because we always had a competition that transcended the actual game score to keep things interesting.

By the way, the Dads beat the Boys 15 to 12. We didn't play in three stadiums as our favorite teams were on the field and we didn't want to root against them. At the beginning, the winners of each game actually received awards. If the boys won, the dads had to buy them jerseys at the respective ballpark's gift shop following the game. If the dads won, the boys had to announce to the entire section that their fathers had superior knowledge of the game and bow to their fathers out of respect. However, as time went on and the competition intensified, bragging rights provided more than enough incentive to win and we disbanded the notion of physical awards.

Another fun game to play is called Ball on the Mound. Here's the deal: At the end of any given inning, the ball rarely finds its way back to the mound. If an outfielder makes the last out, he typically tosses it to a fan on his way into the dugout. Ditto for an infielder (generally a first baseman) making the final out in an inning. In fact, just about the only way the ball will end up on the mound after an inning is if the third out is a strikeout and the catcher rolls the ball to the mound and it stays on the dirt.

Here are the rules: The ball has to be resting on the mound's dirt. Believe it or not, this will only happen a few times per game. The ball has to find its way to the mound via the hands a player, not an umpire (home plate umpires regularly roll balls to the mound to await the next inning's pitcher).

Each side (dads vs boys) selects the top or bottom half of the innings (you need to disqualify the 9th inning because those with the bottom half of the inning could be at a disadvantage as it oftentimes isn't played). You can keep score of how many times the ball ended up on the mound in your half of the inning per game or keep a running competition for the entire trip. You'd be surprised how much fun this little game provides as you'll find yourself screaming to the players on the field to drop the ball on the mound at the end of each inning.

As an aside, a number of people who play this game drop money into a pot each half inning and the winner gets the pot. We didn't want to make gamblers out of our boys, but if you are traveling with adults on your stadium tours, you may want to consider this rule enhancement. Another option is to have the "winner" buy beers for the group each time the ball ends up on the mound in his or her designated half inning.

The important thing is to implement fun activities during each ballgame that make things more exciting and keep your kids engaged. They won't even notice if the real game is boring. There were times we didn't even know the game's final score, but you can bet we knew which side won our own personal competitions!

Make every city an adventure

"The city is the teacher of the man."

—Simondes of Ceos

The ballgames are great. The ballparks are unique and special. But the best memories you'll have will be those created in the large and interesting cities you visit.

Truth is every single city you'll tour has multiple points of interest. Lots of them. When you get to the section later in this book that describes each ballpark, we've included highlights about the market in which it sits. There's a reason for this: You need to explore these wonderful destinations. All of them. Make the time and the commitment because we're willing to bet that neither you nor your kid will ever return to many of these places.

Every market has special interests. And when you look at your map as you drive from city to city, you'll discover sites and destinations worth exploring. As mentioned earlier, we hit the NFL Hall of Fame on our drive from Pittsburgh to Cincinnati. You won't want to miss the NBA Hall of Fame in Springfield, Massachusetts. You can get there by taking the long way from New York to Boston (time permitting). And if you have an open day or two, go to Cooperstown and catch the Baseball Hall of Fame, it's a 3 ½ hour drive from New York City.

Here's the point: This isn't a footrace. The goal isn't to complete the 30 ballparks as quickly as possible (well, maybe it is for some people, but they missed a lot). There's a reason we've referred to these trips as a journey. It's about sharing unique experiences and learning about our history and rich culture. It's about understanding what makes America so darn special by the very nature of its fabric.

Go see a rodeo. Catch a NASCAR race. See outer space from a world class telescope. Watch the Changing of the Guard at the Tomb of the Unknown Soldier. Stand on a glass floor 96 stories above the streets of Chicago. Catch a Broadway Show. Play Nerf football on the sand at South Beach. Sit in the same window as Lee Harvey Oswald on that fateful November day in 1963. Walk across the Golden Gate Bridge and check out the skyline of San Francisco. Watch money being made at the US Mint. Retrace the steps of Paul Revere. Do it all and then some.

This journey will be one you'll share over and over again with your kid for the rest of your life. He'll hopefully share it with his kid. It's special. Milk it for all it's worth. And if that means taking in fewer stadiums per year and spending a day or two extra in each city, so be it. When you're finished, you'll be less interested in the length of the journey than the experiences you shared.

Do it all and do it right and your kid will want to do it every year. Just race from ballpark to ballpark and you'll be missing the point. And you'll risk having a kid whose interest wanes over time.

Chapter 3: How to thoroughly visit a ballpark

Scoring great seats and stadium experiences

Let's face it, the quality of the seats for any given ballgame will impact the overall experience. However, MLB seats have become downright expensive. We witnessed a precipitous increase in ticket pricing over the seven years we toured the stadiums.

While the average cost for a ticket is $25 (and the more popular teams like the Cubs, Yankees and Red Sox are almost twice that amount), according to Team Marketing Report, this figure is extremely misleading. The next time you're at a ballgame, look around the stadium. Most of the seats aren't very desirable. You've got the bleachers (which are typically a 9 iron away from home plate) and the upper deck seats. These two sections take up more than half the tickets available for sale. Assuming you don't want to sit in the nose bleed seats or require a set of binoculars to watch the base runners, you'll want to be on the lower deck in most ballparks. Those seats will average closer to $50 per ticket. And that assumes you don't go for the VIP or similar seats that can cost you a C-Note or more.

In many of the more popular ballparks, you can't even buy the lower level seats from the team website as they are already pre-sold to season ticket holders. You can go to Stubhub.com or another ticket service, but you'll have to pay a premium price, handling costs and mailing fees. It can get pretty pricey in a hurry.

An even more memorable opportunity is to score a private tour of the stadium for your group. You'll learn all kinds of facts that will entirely change your perception of the ballpark. For example, did you know they have a specially designed humidor in Denver for the baseballs used in every game? It turns out the air is so dry the balls were carrying too far and the number of home runs hit in the stadium in the early years became ridiculous. Other teams in both dry and very humid climates are now implementing this humidification strategy in an attempt to normalize the hitting activities. I'm pretty confident this information would have escaped us were it not for the tour of Coors Field. Here's another insight: When you go to Coors Field, all the seats are purple except for a single row around the entire ballpark that is turquoise. Wanna know why? That row of seats is exactly one mile above sea level. Pretty cool stuff that you aren't likely to learn without the benefit of a tour.

There are group tours offered to the public by many teams. They generally cost around $10 per person and we'd highly recommend that you get to the ballpark good and early to take advantage of the tours. Later in the guide, I have provided all sorts of tour information for every ballpark.

Private tours are far more comprehensive and can be personalized. By following a few tips offered herein, you'll probably score a few private tours. And they may be free. Want some better news? They may even include free seats and an on-field experience during batting practice if you get lucky!

Here's the deal: You are no more than six degrees of separation for securing incredible seats and perhaps a private tour of each stadium. You just have to use your wits and your email address book or social media directory.

It turns out most people will get very excited when they hear about your trip. The notion of traveling around the county with your kid or a friend to catch every major league baseball park is just plain heartwarming to most folks. And their natural tendency will be to help you if they possibly can.

You'll be surprised when you find out who has great connections. Some people will connect with ticket owners (corporate or other) via work, others through friends and others will simply pass your request along to their address book and you'll score from people you've never even met.

It can happen a lot if you're willing to invest the time into it. Be sure to inform your email recipients of your plans to visit every single baseball park with your kid. Since this will be a once in a lifetime experience, anything they can do to help secure remarkable seats and/or an on-field experience during batting practice and/or a private stadium tour would be appreciated.

I can practically guarantee you that if you aggressively pursue this strategy, it will pay out in dividends. In several cases, we were able to sit in seats that would otherwise be well beyond our budget constraints or flat out not available at all. We met countless players, grabbed scores of autographs and watched batting practice from the playing fields in St. Louis, Cleveland, NY Mets, Boston, Florida, Colorado and Seattle.

Sometimes the tours were outstanding and led to actually spending quality time with the players. For example, when we were standing in the bullpen at Shea Stadium, Tom Glavine, then a Met, was just hanging out and struck up a conversation with our foursome. He ended up giving our boys pitching tips and reminding them of the life lessons garnered by playing baseball. Talk about a memory! It's safe to say Tom is one of our sons' favorite professional athletes to this day.

In Boston, the boys sat in the Red Sox dugout before the game and actually picked up the phone and called the Bullpen. It doesn't get much cooler than that!

And in Cleveland, the four of us were invited into the Indians' locker room and watched a number of the players taking batting practice on the ball machines under the stadium (we didn't even know ballparks had ball machines available to the players). Jody Gerut, then with the Indians, actually gave the boys some batting tips. He also pointed out the seriously damaged clock on the wall that was destroyed by Albert Belle's fist after a particularly bad game many years ago.

Our boys had the opportunity to see the warm and very human side of professional athletes. When we were in St. Louis for an on-field experience, another kid was on the turf alongside us during batting practice. He had a cast on one leg and was walking with the aid of some crutches. Mike Matheny, the Cardinal's starting catcher at the time, walked over and asked him what happened to his leg. As it turns out, he was in a Little League ballgame and hit a long one to the fence. As he rounded second base, his cleat somehow got stuck in the bag. Suffice it to say, when the rest of his body turned at second base his knee and foot did not. Hence the need for reconstructive surgery, the cast and the long face. Mike asked the boy to stay put (like he had anywhere else to go at that moment!), ran into the dugout, pulled out a bat, signed it and told the kid it wouldn't help his leg get better, but it might cheer him up when he's down in the dumps about his injury. There wasn't a dry eye among us. You read about athletes who are selfish, self-centered and unkind to their adoring public, but it warms your heart when you witness a selfless act like this. It taught our boys a lot about humility, which is, of course, a great life lesson. And this experience wouldn't have happened but for my reaching out and a friend delivering on our behalf.

These types of experiences can happen to you. You just have to make it a priority to aggressively reach out once you've locked down the dates of your games each season. We finalized our plans by mid-January each season and begin our email campaign by February 1st. We'd send another email in mid-March reminding recipients of our upcoming trip and bring them up to date relative to our needs. Since opening day for most teams is in the first week in April, ticket holders will have received their seasons' tickets by then. If we still had ballparks without tickets or experiences for that year's trip, we had plenty of time to order them online either from Stubhub or directly from the each team's website, should all other efforts fail.

Another way to reach out to those with special access to great seats and/or ballpark experiences is via the numerous online social networks. Sending a message across Facebook, Plaxo or Linkedin will reach hundreds or even thousands of possible helpers. One thing is certain: Don't be shy. People love to help because they want to be part of your extraordinary adventure.

If all else fails, go to each team's website and with a bit of noodling around, you will probably find the name of the Director of Community Relations (or a similar title). Each team has one. This person's role in the organization is to reach out to the community in the interest in building good feelings about the team. You'll want to send this person a letter describing your adventure and the date in which you plan to visit their ballpark. Be sure to include pictures of your visits to other ballparks (if possible) to add credibility. You'll almost always get something. Perhaps it'll be a complementary group tour. Sometimes it's coupons for free concessions. Other times it may include an on-field experience. There's absolutely no downside to making contact with the Community Relations Department and they won't be offended. In fact, they are generally pleased to accommodate you.

As an example, here is a copy of the letter I sent to the Community Relations Department for the Seattle Mariners. You'll obviously want to personalize it to fit your writing style and your group's wishes.

April 2, 2009

Ms. Gina Hasson
Director of Community Relations
Seattle Mariners
Safeco Field
1250 First Avenue South
Seattle, WA 98134

Dear Gina,

My son and I, along with another father-son team, have spent part of the past 5 summers visiting major league baseball parks. The four of us (our sons are now 13) have visited 26 parks and will be visiting Safeco Field on Saturday, May 23rd.

As you probably know, baseball is the only professional sport where the field of play differs in each park. Every stadium has its own personality and each deserves to be explored to the fullest.

That brings me to the purpose of this letter. We've been blessed by many of your counterparts at other MLB parks who have been willing to arrange for tours, batting practice on-field experiences and/or extraordinary seats. I would like to ask if it would be possible for you to put together something on our behalf. The four of us would be forever indebted to you for your generosity.

I have attached some images of the four of us at other MLB ballparks in the hope that you will share our enthusiasm for this remarkable journey. Hopefully, you can help optimize the quality of our experience at Safeco Field.

Please feel free to contact me at your earliest convenience. The easiest place to reach me is at my office (number and email on the letterhead).

I want to thank you, in advance, for your help in making our evening at Safeco a memorable one. I look forward to hearing from you soon.

Sincerely,
Stan Fridstein

This particular letter was quite effective. We were able to secure a remarkable private stadium tour that took us to the owner's box, on the field during batting practice, into the dugout and into the bowels of the stadium that are usually seen only by employees, players and coaches. It was a remarkable experience that lasted for well over an hour.

As for securing great seats, here is a word of advice: You don't have tickets until you have them in your hot little hands. There were several occasions when we were promised tickets that never arrived. In the meantime, we declined offers for great seats at those stadiums on the assumption our search was complete. You're far better off having more than one set of tickets and returning the unused ones to their original owners than ending up without those great seats that would be otherwise unattainable at a reasonable price (if at all).

One final thought on this subject that will be invaluable as you go forward. The people who help you in the beginning of your journey will oftentimes be the same folks who are well connected and will aid your efforts down the road. Be sure to always send a thank you note along with pictures of your group at the ballpark in which they provided your tickets and/or experiences. It's a little thing, but it just makes sense. It also reinforces their enthusiasm for the experience they helped to craft.

Chapter 4: Experience the Ballpark and the City

You will spend the minority of your time in the ballparks. Think about it, even if you get to the ballpark when the gates open (generally about 90 minutes before game time) and stay until the last out, you'll rarely be there for more than five hours. This means the majority of your time will be spent either traveling between cities and/or exploring the cities that house MLB teams.

We spent quite a bit of time researching things to do in each city that would appeal to adults and kids on the trip and I'm happy to share this wealth of knowledge with you.

A few caveats are in order. We visited the stadiums over a seven year period. Some prices and policies may have changed at every venue (city and stadium). Be sure to visit the websites of any activities that are of interest to secure the most current information.

There are numerous books that describe the ballparks in painfully excruciating detail, and there is no need to repeat the information in this book. This book is not intended to regurgitate ballpark statistics, famous plays, and events. You can find that online and in many existing tomes. There are also beautifully designed books with luscious photographs of the stadiums. They are made to sit on coffee tables. This book has been written as a working guide that will follow you into each market and stadium. It ain't pretty, but I think you'll find it to be useful.

Provided herein are interesting tid-bits of information that will help you to enjoy the stadiums. I've identified things you won't want to miss. You'll find little known facts, secrets, and other pieces of information that we learned on our tours or via our own comprehensive research in the hope of making each experience that much more special.

The stadium information tends to focus on the physical structure rather than providing an historical perspective of the players, managers and games/series. Again, the idea is to help you to walk around each and every stadium and locate the most interesting sights, sounds and activities available to you. And be sure to get to the games as early as possible and explore to your heart's content. Too many fans simply grab a hot dog and head to their seats. Frankly, they are missing out on the special aspects each stadium has to offer. See it all and take it in. A tremendous amount of thought has gone into each stadium and much of it is extremely subtle.

As for the order of this section, the cities have been bunched into geographic sections based on the assumption that you'll be visiting the cities in the most efficient manner. While you certainly won't hit the geographic sections (or the cities within that section) in the same order we did, I knew of no better way to present the information. There is an index in the front of the book that provides easily accessible page numbers for each city so you won't have to flail through the book in search of each destination.

I have also listed the street address for each stadium because you may elect to use a GPS system and will want this information. We always used one and it was invaluable.

Midwestern Cities and Stadiums
Chicago
Things to do in Chicago:

Lincoln Park Zoo: This wonderful zoo offers up a world of wildlife in the shadow of Chicago's skyscrapers. Located just minutes north of the city center (we walked to the zoo on the boardwalk that runs alongside Lake Michigan), the zoo has been a natural oasis for generations of animal lovers. It's free. For more information: http://www.lpzoo.com.

John Hancock Building Observatory: (875 N. Michigan Avenue). Cool views of the entire city and the opportunity to see four states (Michigan, Wisconsin, Illinois and Indiana). Tickets are about $15 per person and worth it. You can even step out on the open air skywalk that takes you on the edge of the building 96 floors above the street (you can't fall thanks to the heavy duty stainless steel screen, but it's pretty harrowing nevertheless). For more information: www.hancock-observatory.com/

The Original Pancake House: (22 East Bellevue, Chicago, Illinois 60611): Feeling a bit too healthy and in need of an over-the-top breakfast? The OPH's signature meal is the Apple Pancake, a single large pancake smothered with sautéed apples and cinnamon sugar and baked to perfection. This is a Chicago institution. Split your meal as the portions are large for even the biggest appetite (what's more, you're going to want to save room for those great Chicago-style hot dogs at the game). For more information: http://www.originalpancakehouse.com/

Museum of Science and Industry: You'll need a cab or car to get to this incredible hands-on museum. It has loads of exhibits and lots of things for kids to do. Come early in the morning and stay all day if you can. You cannot possibly see everything at the museum in a short period of time. Don't miss the Coal Mine or U505 Submarine (an actual Nazi sub captured during WWII). Admission starts at $13 for adults and $9 for kids. For more information: http://www.msichicago.org/

Pizzeria Uno and Pizzeria Due: This is the home of the original deep dish pizza for which Chicago has become synonymous and it's still the best. Both restaurants share the same ownership and are located a block from one another (you can walk to either from downtown). Do yourself a favor: Do not look at the nutritional breakdown offered on their website as you consider which deep dish pizza you're going to consider. Let's just say your meal will be in the thousands of calories and leave it at that. It's worth every extra pound. For more information: http://www.unos.com/great.html.

Navy Pier: For well over a decade, Navy Pier has been a central location for fun in Chicago. Located right on the lake (it was actually a military pier in its youth, hence the name), it offers up loads of restaurants, entertainment, rides and more. It's an easy walk from Michigan Avenue. If you're traveling with young kids, there's a children's museum. You can even rent Segways there and take your own tour of Chicago. For more information: http://www.navypier.com/about/about_us.html

Take a kayak tour of the city: Experience Chicago's magnificent architecture and history from the peaceful platform of a sea kayak. Thousands of visitors have kayaked their way up and down the Chicago River on their guided tour. It's located in the heart of the city and promises to leave you with incredible memories as you get a duck's eye view. Tours are about 3 hours long and cost $55 per person. If you are an experienced kayaker and want to paddle on your own, you can rent a kayak for as little as $15 an hour. For more information: http://www.wateriders.com/.

Wendella Boat Tour: These people offer the city's most comprehensive tours from the water. There are architectural tours, city tours and more, all from the comfort of large boats. Depending on the tour, you'll be on the Chicago River and/or Lake Michigan. The tours depart from the Wrigley Building on Michigan Avenue, so you can walk to the boat launch if you're staying downtown. Ticket prices vary by tour, but they are about $23 for adults and $13 for kids. For more information: http://www.wendellaboats.com/tours.htm.

Oak Street Beach: Oak Street Beach, just north of the Magnificent Mile and Michigan Avenue, is one of Chicago's most popular spots. It's is a haven to inline skaters, cyclists, volleyball enthusiasts and, of course, sunbathers. The sandy beach is wide and the concrete areas at either side are also popular for sunbathing and people-watching. There are concessions and restrooms, but no parking. At the south end of the beach, the Oak Street Beachstro (get it?) serves steak, pastas, seafood, salads and sandwiches.

Chicago Cubs

Park Name: Wrigley Field
Address: 1060 West Addison, Chicago, IL 60613
Capacity: 41,118
Opening Day: April 23, 1914 (the Chicago Federals played there for two years). The original opening day for the Chicago Cubs was April 20, 1916)
Dimensions (feet):

Left Field- 355
Center Field- 400
Right Field- 353
Cheapest seat: $8
Most Expensive seat: $315
Stadium Tours: A tour of Wrigley Field provides an insider's look at more than 90 years of history in this legendary ballpark. The tour stops include the Cubs clubhouse, visitor's clubhouse, dugouts, on-deck circles, press box, bleachers and mezzanine suites. The total length is about an hour and a half, so be sure to wear comfortable clothing and shoes. Tours depart from Gate D (located at the corner of Addison Street and Sheffield Avenue) every half hour. You'll want to arrive at least 15 minutes prior to your tour time. To reserve a tour, go to CUBS.com or call 773-404-CUBS. Tour tickets are $25 each. It's not cheap, but this is Wrigley Field, after all!

Some interesting information about Wrigley Field:

◈ Wrigley Field is the second-oldest ballpark in the majors behind Boston's Fenway Park (1912). Originally known as Weeghman Park, Wrigley Field was built on the grounds once occupied by a seminary. The park became known as Cubs Park in 1920 after the Wrigley family purchased the team from the Weeghman family. It was renamed Wrigley Field in 1926 in honor of William Wrigley Jr., the club's owner.

◈ Talk about inflation: The new Yankees Stadium was built at an estimated cost of $1.3 billion. Compare that with the cost of building Wrigley Field: $250,000.

◈ No batted ball has ever hit the centerfield scoreboard ... two baseballs barely missed - a homer hit onto Sheffield

Avenue (right-center) by Bill Nicholson in 1948, and one hit by Roberto Clemente onto Waveland Avenue (left-center) in 1959. Of interest, Sam Snead did manage to hit the big board with a golf ball teed off from home plate.

◇ Ever since 1937, a flag with either a "W" or an "L" has flown from atop the scoreboard masthead, indicating the day's result. In case a doubleheader is split, both flags are flown. A white flag with a blue "W" indicates a victory; a blue flag with a white "L" denotes a loss. There are also other flags that indicate where the Cubs are in the standings.

◇ Wrigley Field is famous for its outfield walls which are covered by ivy. The ivy was planted in 1937 by then Cubs General Manager Bill Veeck, who would later become the owner of the Chicago White Sox. In the first weeks of the baseball season, the ivy has not leafed out, and all that is visible are the vines on which it grows. However, as the season progresses further into spring, the ivy grows thick and green, disguising the hard brick surface of the outfield wall. You may very well see a ball get lost in the ivy when hit towards the outfield fences. An outfielder will signal a lost ball, by raising his hands. When this occurs, the umpires will call time and rule the play a ground rule double. But get this: If the player attempts to search for the ball, the play is considered live, and no ground-rule double is ruled.

◇ Take a look at the foul poles. Ernie Banks' uniform No. 14 and Ron Santo's No. 10 are imprinted on flags which fly from the leftfield foul pole ... Billy Williams' No. 26 and Ryne Sandberg's No. 23 fly from the right field foul pole.

❖ Lights for Wrigley Field were originally to be installed for the 1942 season. However because of the United States' involvement in World War II after the bombing of Pearl Harbor, Phil Wrigley donated the lights to the government for the war effort. After 5,687 consecutive day games played by the Cubs at Wrigley, the lights were finally lit on August 8, 1988, a very sad day for many Cubs fans.

❖ Talk about working it both ways. The custom of allowing fans to keep foul balls hit into the stands started at Wrigley Field. However, the custom of throwing a home run ball hit by opposing players back onto the field also started here.

❖ Sadly, the Cubs have never won a World Series title at Wrigley Field, having lost in all six attempts since 1918. Their last world championship came in 1908, six years before Wrigley was built.

❖ The famous "Bleacher Bums" were formed here in 1966 by 10 fans.

❖ The Cubs have been blessed with two of the most legendary broadcasters of all time. Don't miss the seven foot tall statue of Harry Caray at the corner of Addison Street and Sheffield Avenue near Gate D, or Jack Brickhouse's trademark "Hey, Hey" cheer that has been placed above the distance markers on both foul pole screens.

❖ Wrigley Field is nicknamed *The Friendly Confines*, by "Mr. Cub", Hall of Famer Ernie Banks.

❖ In April and May the wind often comes off Lake Michigan (less than a mile to the east), which means a northeast wind "blowing in" can knock down potential home runs and turn them into outs. In the summer, however, or on any warm and breezy day, the wind often comes from the south and the southwest, which means the wind is "blowing out" and has the potential to turn normally harmless fly balls into home runs. This makes Wrigley one of the most unpredictable parks in the Major Leagues.

◈ The scoreboard is still manually operated (only Fenway provides the same labor intensive score reporting system). A number turner has scores from around MLB fed to him via computer, and updates this by manually replacing the numbers from within the scoreboard. The scoreboard is made out of sheet steel. The numbers that are placed into the inning windows are steel, painted forest green, and numbered with white numerals. The box for the game playing at Wrigley uses yellow numerals to indicate the current inning. The clock, which sits at the top center of the scoreboard, has never lost time in its 69-year existence.

◈ For years, a ritual of each game involved announcer Harry Caray singing "Take Me Out To The Ballgame" (very off key) during the 7th Inning Stretch. Ever since Harry Caray passed away, the Cubs have invited a celebrity to lead the crowd in singing this time-honored song.

◈ Stay until the end of the game, even if the Cubs are winning big. You'll be treated to the Cubs anthem, *Go Cubs Go*, which is sung by the crowd after every win. The song was written in 1983 by dying fan Steve Goodman and adopted as a stadium staple in 2007. There's nothing like it anywhere else in baseball.

◈ To take in the full Wrigley Field experience, here's one ritual you won't want to miss. Get to the game early, stand on Waveland Avenue and battle with the ball hawks as they scramble for home runs hit out of the park during batting practice. It's a hoot!

Chicago White Sox

Park Name: U.S. Cellular Field
Address: 333 West 35th Street, Chicago, IL 60616
Capacity: 40,615
Opening Day: April 18, 1991
Dimensions (feet):
Left Field- 330
Center Field- 400
Right Field- 335
Cheapest seat: $10
Most Expensive seat: $100
Stadium Tours: Unfortunately, U.S. Cellular Field tours are only available for groups of 10 or more. The tours run on Tuesdays and Fridays - 10:30 a.m. on game days and 10:30 a.m. and 1:30 p.m. on non-game days. Tours include the home dugout, the press box, the field, the suites and the Stadium Club. Advance reservations are required. For details and rates, call 312-674-1000.

Some interesting information about U.S. Cellular Field:

◈ The dirt on the infield of U.S. Cellular Field was transported from the old Comiskey Park, home of the White Sox from 1910 until they moved into the current stadium in 1991.

◈ U.S. Cellular Park was the last MLB stadium built before the wave of new retro-classic ballparks became the rage in the 1990's and 2000's.

◈ The "exploding scoreboard" in center field pays homage to the original installed by Bill Veeck, former owner, at the old Comiskey Park in 1960.

◈ Don't miss the White Sox Champions Brick Plaza outside the ballpark's main entrance. Each brick is inscribed with a personalized message that has become part of a new baseball diamond-shaped plaza. Proceeds from the sale of the legacy bricks went to White Sox charities. It was so successful the organization has announced details for the second round of brick sales.

◈ You can actually have a patio party at U.S. Cellular Field. Groups of 20 or more can get an all-you-can-eat buffet of burgers, hot dogs, chicken, BBQ ribs, salads, wine, beer and soda before any game. It costs $20 to $41 per person, but you also get a discount of $5 to $10 on your game tickets. The food is decent and you can watch the teams warm up from the outfield patios before you go to your seats. It's kind of like tailgating inside the park!

◈ Let's face it, for most guys, going to a ballgame isn't complete without throwing down a few beers. Both the lower and upper decks at U.S. Cellular Park have "Beers of the World" stands where you can get high-quality domestic and imported beers. Their selections include Honey Brown, Tecate, Guinness, Stella Artois, Heineken, Bell's Oberon, Pilsner Urquell and much more. Drink up, boys!

◈ While U.S. Cellular Field is only 19 years old, not very long in baseball terms, the White Sox have done a decent job of instilling a sense of history at the ballpark. There's a very cool sculpture outside Gate 4 honoring the 2005 World Series Championship. It includes depictions of most of the Series' best moments, from Paul Konerko's grand slam in Game 2 to Scott Podsednik's Game 2 winning homer. There's plenty more nostalgia to soak in once you get inside. Along the outfield concourse, you'll find statues of some of the team's best players, including Carlton Fisk, Harold Baines, Nellie Fox, Luis Aparicio, Billy Pierce and Minnie Minoso.

◈ Although nearly every seat in the stadium was replaced with a green seat in 2006 and 2007, two of the original blue seats remain. Those seats are where Paul Konerko hit his grand slam in Game 2 and where Scott Podsednik hit his Game 2 walk-off homer in the 2005 World Series.

◈ It's not often I'll send you to the parking lot to see something special. However, in Lot B, you'll find home plate from old Comiskey Park embedded in the blacktop in its original location.

◈ The Sox Shower, located in left-center field, is a place to go to cool off during hot summer day games. It's an actual shower, and, depending on the temperature and humidity, it may be a welcome sight!

◈ An important thing to consider when you buy your tickets: Your ticket can only get you to your portion of the stadium. If you have an upper deck seat, you're stuck in the upper deck; you can't go anywhere else in the stadium. So if this is your first time U.S. Cellular Park, you'll miss out on walking the entire stadium if you don't have great seats. We believe this to be the only ballpark designed in this fashion.

Milwaukee
Things to do in Milwaukee:

The Harley-Davidson Museum: If you only have time for one activity in this city and you're with your son, he'll never forgive if you pass up on this wonderful experience. The museum celebrates the passion, people, products and culture of everything that is Harley-Davidson. Check out the very first Harley-Davidson motorcycle, see how these bad boys are built and learn the history of the ultimate two wheel icon. Don't even think of walking out of the gift shop empty handed! Admission to the museum is $16 for adults and $10 for kids. For more information: www.harley-davidson.com.

Miller Brewery: Milwaukee Brewery, one of the world's largest, sits on land originally purchased by Frederick J. Miller in 1855. Some 800 employees work round-the-clock, producing 10 million barrels of beer per year. The brewery offers free, one-hour indoor/outdoor guided walking tours, where visitors witness each step of the brewing process. The tours, starting at the Visitor Center located at 4251 W. State St., include a stop in the Historic Caves and conclude at the Bavarian-Style Miller Inn, where you can relax and enjoy a frosty beer sample (if you're 21 or older...but your underage kid can still tour). Tours are generally available from 10:30 a.m. to 3:30 p.m. Monday through Saturday. For more information, call 414-931-BEER.

Milwaukee County Zoo: The Milwaukee County Zoo is a serene home to more than 1,800 mammals, birds, fish, amphibians and reptiles with more than 350 species represented on 200 acres of beautiful parkland. It's considered to be one of the best zoos in the country. For more information: http://www.milwaukeezoo.org/.

Usinger's Sausage Factory Tour: Here's an opportunity to grab an exclusive, behind-the-scenes tour of one of America's premier sausage factories. It's located on the site of the original store that opened in 1880 (1030 N. Old World Third St.). Feinschmecker's (sausage gourmets, but you already knew that) will find about 70 varieties of old world sausage. Whether you're looking for bratwurst or beerwurst, the superior German-style wurst made and served here doesn't get any better than this. For more information: http://www.usinger.com/info.php.

Milwaukee Brewers

Park Name: Miller Park
Address: One Brewers Way, Milwaukee, WI 53214
Capacity: 42,400
Opening Day: April 6, 2001
Dimensions (feet):
Left Field- 344
Center Field- 400
Right Field- 345
Cheapest seat: $8
Most Expensive seat: $68
Stadium Tours: Experience Miller Park via a tour that includes the dugout, luxury suite level, visiting clubhouse, press box, Bob Uecker's broadcast booth and other behind-the-scenes attractions. Tours meet outside the Brewers Team Store in Miller Park's Hot Corner down the left field line. Tours cover about a 1/2 mile and last approximately 70 minutes. The tour route is wheelchair and stroller friendly. Tour Hotline is 414-902-4005 or visit the Brewers' website. Price: $10 for adults and $6 for kids.

Some interesting information about Miller Park:

◇ If you're into baseball history, don't miss the Walk of Fame at Miller Park. Located on the Plaza area outside the park, the Walk of Fame commemorates some of the most famous players in Brewers and Braves history with granite home plates set into the ground. Remember Cecil Cooper? He's there alongside Bob Uecker, Gorman Thomas, Harvey Kuenn, Eddie Matthews, Warren Spahn and several others. There are also statues of greats Robin Yount and Hank Aaron.

◇ As you approach Miller Park, the most impressive site has to be the retractable roof. The 12,000 ton, seven panel roof has a unique fan shape design. It can open or close in ten minutes and sits 175 feet above the playing field. The retractable roof was built in a unique convertible style, with the roof panels opening and closing simultaneously in a sweeping manner from the first- and third-base sides toward center field. This enables the seating area to be heated 30 degrees warmer than the outside temperature when closed, allowing games to be played in more comfortable conditions than an open air stadium. This is somewhat important, given Wisconsin's often cool weather conditions early and late in the season. In fact, the roof is closed if game temperatures are expected to drop below 60 degrees, or if rain or high winds are in the forecast.

◇ Miller Park is the only major league ballpark that sells more sausages than it does hot dogs. That's something to consider when you're thinking about your choice of main courses during a Brewers' game.

◈ Paying homage to the Brewer's former stadium, the grass playing surface consists mostly of sod transplanted from the old County Stadium.

◈ Don't think of getting out of your seat in the middle of the 6th inning or you'll miss the famous Sausage Race. The current "racing sausages" are the Bratwurst, Italian, Chorizo, Polish and Hot Dog. There are imitations of this race at other stadiums, but nothing matches the amusement generated by these doggies.

◈ How many baseballs would it take to fill Miller Park up to the top of the roof? The Brewers claim the number exceeds 4.6 billion. Want some additional trivia? It would take 62 million 16 pound bowling balls to equal the weight of the Miller Park structure.

◈ If a Brewer hits a home run, immediately fix your eyes on the left field seats, where Bernie Brewer, the team mascot, will make a splash in the "Kalahari Splash Zone" area, sending an explosion of water into the air. Bernie Brewer also hits the water if the Brewers win the game.

◈ During the seventh inning stretch, in addition to "Take me out to the Ballgame", fans at Miller Park sing the "Beer Barrel Polka". You won't hear that song anywhere else in the majors.

◈ The field dimensions were designed with the input of Robin Yount, who played his entire 20-year career with the Brewers. It's not too surprising that this is a hitters' park. For example, take a good look at the outfield fences. There are a number of weird and very sharp angles. This makes for some interesting shots off the wall and extra base hits. You can tell a pitcher had no input on this design!

St. Louis
Things to do in St. Louis

The Gateway Arch- The Arch has been a popular tourist attraction since its completion in October 1965. Designed to last 1,000 years, it reaches 630 feet in height as it stands next to the Mississippi River. On a clear day, you can see for about 30 miles from atop the structure. You travel up one of the two trams that bend around the arch's interior. It's a bit claustrophobic but memorable ride, complete with some informative narration. It's a must see if you have a few extra minutes and there's nothing like it anywhere else in the world. Admission is $7 for adults and $5 for kids. For more information: http://www.gatewayarch.com/Arch/.

The St. Louis Zoo: This is the third-largest zoo in the country, with 90 acres of space and 700 species of animals on exhibit. Be sure to check out Big Cat country, the Jungle of the Apes, the Primate House, the River's Edge (an elephant exhibit) and feeding areas for bears and sea lions. Free general admission. For more information: http://www.stlzoo.org/.

Grant's Farm: In the 1850s, Ulysses S. Grant began farming this land, now a tourist attraction and a home to many exotic and endangered animals. Grant's Farm offers visitors numerous activities, from touring the land and seeing the animals to attending the shows and dining. Anheuser-Busch owns the farm, which is home to the Clydesdale stables. Grant's Station and Grant's Cabin are two of the major attractions on the tour. Admission is free. For more information: www.grantsfarm.com.

St. Louis Cardinals

Park Name: Busch Stadium
Address: 700 Clark Avenue, St. Louis, MO 63102
Capacity: 46,700
Opening Day: April 10, 2006
Dimensions (feet):
Left Field- 336
Center Field- 400
Right Field- 335
Cheapest seat: $19
Most Expensive seat: $250
Stadium Tours: Tours include the Redbird Club, the Press Box, the Cardinals Club, the Cardinals Dugout, and a few other unique areas in the ballpark. The tours are offered daily throughout the baseball season when a night game is scheduled. There are a few exceptions, so you'll want to contact the tour office at (314) 345-9565 or stadiumtours@stlcardinals.com. Tour tickets can be purchased at Gate 5 ticket windows 19 and 20 on Clark Street (on the north side of the ballpark). The tour ticket office opens 30 minutes prior to the first tour and tickets are only available on the day the tour is offered. Tours are offered at 9:30am, 11:00am, 12:30pm, and 2:00pm. Cost: $10 for adults and $6 for kids.

Some interesting information about Busch Stadium:

◈ When you enter the ballpark, one of the first things that will grab you is the breathtaking view beyond the outfield seats...you get to see the skyline of downtown St. Louis and the Gateway Arch.

◈ The Cardinals became the first team since the New York Yankees in 1923 to win the World Series the same year they opened Busch Stadium in 2006.

◈ This is the third stadium in St. Louis to carry the Busch name. Sportsman's Park was renamed Busch Stadium in 1953, after team owner Gussie Busch. In 1966, both the baseball and football Cardinals moved to a new multipurpose stadium, under the same moniker. By the way, Busch Stadium was the first baseball stadium to be named after a corporate sponsor (even if the sponsor also owned the team).

◈ A walk around the outside of the stadium will bring you to some statues, including one of Stan Musial along 8th Street. And the Jack Bucks bust is just beyond the center field wall. Take some time to look at the top 100 Cardinal moments that are etched into marble plaques, surrounded by fan-sponsored bricks as you walk the exterior of Busch Stadium. Also, don't miss the markers on the sidewalks surrounding the stadium signifying where the outfield was in Old Busch. That's because the new stadium was actually built into the old one (the final piece was completed during the off season in 2005-2006).

◈ Be sure to enter the stadium through Gate 3, behind third base. They designed a gateway for the ages, using the Eads Bridge, a beautiful bridge that spans the Mississippi River just beyond the stadium, as its inspiration. It is a remarkable way to be introduced to Busch. Not long after passing the entrance at Gate 3, you'll encounter the immense rotunda at the home-plate entry and that is a sight to behold as well.

◈ Take a look at the dugouts and you'll spot the pennants won by the Cardinals over the years. The retired numbers are located just beneath the scoreboard.

◈ If you feel like eating some ballpark food, you're not alone. They sell 540,000 hot dogs, 181,000 pounds of nacho chips and 32,000 gallons of nacho cheese per season. So don't worry, it's unlikely they'll run out any time soon.

◈ Here's some trivia (like the number of gallons of nacho cheese dished out per season isn't trivia!): There are approximately 3,000 day-of-game employees at Busch Stadium.

◈ For some pre-game fun, take a stroll to the Ford Family Plaza, where you can catch performers entertaining the crowd. There are also some shops and one will even craft a baseball bat custom-made for you (bring your charge card!).

◈ More fun is available at the U.S. Cellular Family Pavilion. It features speed-pitch and batting cage. The top level of this Pavilion houses the Coca-Cola Scoreboard Patio where for about a C-Note, you can watch the game from this elevated perch and eat and drink all you want.

Kansas City
Things to do in Kansas City

Negro Leagues Baseball Museum- No real baseball fan can afford to miss this museum. Racism and "Jim Crow" laws forced black players to form their own units, "barnstorming" around the country to play anyone who would challenge them. In 1920, an organized league structure was formed. In a meeting held in Kansas City, a few team owners joined to form the Negro National League, bringing the thrills and innovative play of black baseball to major urban centers and rural country-sides. The last Negro League teams folded in the early 1960s (well after Jackie Robinson broke the color barrier in Major League Baseball and paved the way for others), but the legacy lives on through the surviving players and the Negro Leagues Baseball Museum. The museum features multi-media computer stations, film exhibits, hundreds of photographs, a field of 12 bronze sculptures and a growing collection of baseball artifacts. For more information: http://www.nlbm.com

The College Basketball Experience: The College Basketball Experience is a high-energy, remarkably-interactive venue where casual and hard core fans can totally immerse themselves in the game of college hoops. This 41,500-square-foot building features the National Collegiate Basketball Hall of Fame. Here, visitors learn about the great players and coaches who have made significant contributions to men's collegiate basketball. You'll be invited to relive seminal moments in college basketball history. Hands-on exhibits throughout the facility place visitors in game-like situations, from sinking the game-winning shot to announcing the play-by-play action from the ESPNU broadcast desk. For more information: http://www.collegebasketballexperience.com

Kansas City Royals

Park Name: Kauffman Stadium
Address: 1 Royal Way, Kansas City, MO 64141
Capacity: 40,793
Opening Day: April 10, 1973
Dimensions (feet):
Left Field- 330
Center Field- 400
Right Field- 330
Cheapest seat: $7
Most Expensive seat: $240
Stadium Tours: The Royals offer a behind-the-scenes peek at Kauffman Stadium via a 75 minute tour which includes Royals Hall of Fame, the Press Box, Royals Interview Room, Royals Dugout and Visitors' Clubhouse (when available). On the days of evening games only the 9:30, 11:00 and 12:30 tours will be available. Tours are not available on day-game days. Prices are from $7 (kids) to $10 (adults). Other tours are available as well. For tour reservations or information either go to the Royal's website or call (816) 504-4222.

Some interesting information about Kauffman Stadium:

◈ The park's best-known feature is the fountain and water-fall display (known as the Water Spectacular) behind the right-field fence. It is the largest privately-funded fountain in the world. The fountains are on display before and after the game and in-between innings, while the waterfalls are constantly flowing. It's not surprising that Kauffman Stadium would feature such a fountain. Kansas City has been building them since 1899 and today boasts of more than 200. The only city in the world with more is Rome.

◈ Every seat in the stadium is blue except for one. Check out the red seat behind home plate. It was placed there to honor former occupant Buck O'Neil, a first baseman and star of the Kansas City Monarchs of the old Negro League. Buck was also the first African American coach in major league baseball. He was also instrumental in founding the Negro Leagues Baseball Museum in Kansas City. A person is selected every game from community nominees to sit in that seat, formerly occupied by O'Neil behind home plate.

◈ Enter the park through Home Plate Gate C and you'll see a walkway with "legacy bricks," as the team calls them. Made of bluestone, numerous personalized bricks surround much larger ones engraved with great moments in Royals history. Pricing for fans that want to be a part of the legacy starts at $150 for a 4" x 8" brick. All monies are donated to charities.

◈ If you walk around the park before the game, don't miss the Outfield Experience. It's full of games and activities for youngsters to enjoy and book-ended by two buildings: the Royals Hall of Fame and Rivals Sports Bar, both providing entertainment for older fans.

◈ It's impossible to miss the crown-shaped scoreboard. Standing 104 feet tall and measuring 84 feet wide, the high-definition scoreboard is an 8,736 square foot behemoth, and when it was unveiled on Opening Day of 2008 it was the largest high-def LED display in the world (only the Dallas Cowboy's new scoreboard has a larger high-def LED display). A staff of 17 is needed to operate it!

◈ Bronze sculptures of George Brett, Dick Howser and Frank White reside upon the outfield concourse in right-center. Text on all four sides of each statue's base tells about the careers of the only three men to have their number retired by the Royals.

◈ The stadium is named for Ewing Kauffman, owner of the Royals from 1969-1993 and a major icon in Kansas City. This is the only stadium in the American League named in honor of a person and just one of three in Major League Baseball (Turner Field and Wrigley Field are the others).

◈ If the game you attend is on a weekend, don't head to the bathroom in the middle of the fourth inning! A live "Hot Dog Derby" takes place, wherein three people in oversized weenie costumes dash down the first base warning track for the glory of finishing first. On second thought, maybe relieving one's self is a better option...

Minneapolis
Things to do in Minneapolis:

Mall of America: We would generally not send you to a mall, with one exception: Mall of America. It's not exclusively about shopping (although there are more than 500 stores). It's really an enormous entertainment world under one roof. There are 20 restaurants, 14 movie theatres and attractions like Nickelodeon Universe, Underwater Adventures Aquarium, LEGO Imagination Center, Dinosaur Walk Museum, A.C.E.S. Flight Simulation, and NASCAR Silicon Motor Speedway. This monster mall has 4.3 miles under roof. For more information: http://www.mallofamerica.com

St. Paul Saints: This hugely popular minor league team draws nearly 300,000 fans each year to its 6,000-seat Midway Stadium. With an eclectic ownership group including baseball maverick Mike Veeck and actor/comedian Bill Murray, the Saints have adopted a "Fun is Good" attitude. Known for their outlandish promotions, the Saints are the only team in baseball with a live pig as its mascot (in 2008 the pig was named Boarack Ohama – past swines have included Hammy Davis, Jr., Notorious P.I.G., Garrison Squeallor and Kevin Bacon), an 80 year-old nun who gives massages in the stands, and haircuts behind home plate. Tickets start at just $4 for kids and $5 for adults. The team has featured many stars in the past including Darryl Strawberry, Jack Morris, J.D. Drew and Kevin Millar. This is the best value in town! For more information: http://www.saintsbaseball.com/home/.

Minnesota Twins

Park Name: Target Field
Address: 1 Twins Way, Minneapolis, MN
Capacity: 39,504

Opening Day: April 12, 2010
Dimensions (feet):
Left Field- 377
Center Field- 411
Right Field- 328
Cheapest seat: $11
Most Expensive seat: $275
Stadium Tours: Target Field Tours are scheduled every Monday through Saturday on non-game days only. There are 4 scheduled tours on each Monday-Saturday non-game day. All tours begin at the Twins Clubhouse Store located at Gate # 29 near the 7th Street side of the ballpark. Tours last approximately 50 minutes. You'll see the Twins' dugout, visit the Champions' Club where the World Series Trophies reside, stand in the press box and much more. Advance reservations are recommended as tours tend to sell-out. Tickets are available online (go to the Twins website), at the ticket box office near Gate 29, or by calling 1-800-33-TWINS. Ticket prices: Adults $15, kids $7.

Some interesting information about Target Field:

◈ The gates at the stadium are numbered after the retired numbers worn by Twins players, in addition to #42, retired throughout Major League Baseball for Jackie Robinson. The center field gate is Gate #3, named for Harmon Killebrew, the left field gate is Gate #6 honoring Tony Oliva, the home plate gate is Gate #14 for Kent Hrbek, the right field gate serves as Gate #29 in tribute to Rod Carew and the plaza gate is known as Gate #34, honoring Kirby Puckett.

◈ Check out the Town Ball Tavern", whose flooring behind the bar is the actual wood surface from the Minneapolis Armory, where the Minneapolis Lakers played before moving to Los Angeles.

◈ Target Field's footprint is only 8.5 acres large – the smallest in Major League Baseball.

◈ The live turf was grown at Graff's Turf Farms, Inc. in Fort Morgan, Colorado. This is the same grass that can be found at Wrigley Field and Notre Dame's Football Stadium. It was shipped to Target Field in 19 refrigerated trucks, and installed within 24 hours of being cut. The turf is heated to about 40 degrees in the winter to keep it in tip top shape for the season.

◈ Target Field has a facade that was built with more than 100,000 square feet of limestone from southwest Minnesota.

◈ Many of the restaurants and food stands feature items that are unique to Minnesota, like the Walleye on a Stick, a Minnesota State Fair favorite.

◈ In Center Field you'll see a caricature of two guys shaking hands in front of a baseball. Their names: Minnie and Paul, taken from the names of the twin cities.

◈ Target Field has earned the title of greenest ballpark in Major League Baseball, and it wasn't by accident. The U.S. Green Building Council awarded Target Field LEED Silver Certification, making it the second MLB ballpark in the United States to achieve that status. Nationals Park, home of the Washington Nationals, is the other ballpark with LEED Silver Certification, however, Target Field collected the most certification points ever awarded a ballpark.

Mideast/Canadian Cities and Stadiums
Toronto:
Things to do in Toronto:

Hockey Hall of Fame: Hey, you may be on a baseball trip, but there are other sports! This interactive center allows you to take shots at real-time goalies, stop shots by Gretzky and Messier, call the play-by-play of some of hockey's greatest moments, view flicks in one of the theatres and get close up to the Stanley Cup. The Hockey Hall of Fame contains the largest collection of hockey memorabilia in the world. For more information: http://www.hhof.com.

Center Island: The Toronto Islands have always been a haven for those who want an afternoon away from the concrete and noise of the city. A twenty minute ferry ride takes you from the dock at the bottom of Bay Street to one of three linked islands. Center Island is where most people go – it has snack bars, picnic areas and a children's amusement park. For more information: http://www.toronto.ca/parks/island/#centre

CN Tower: The tallest building in the world is a must-see for visitors: On a clear day, the view from the observation deck on the top of the tower extends all the way to Niagara Falls. Go late in the day when the city lights come on and the lines thin out. When was the last time you stood on a glass floor 100+ stories above the ground? We thought so. For more information: www.cntower.ca

Toronto Blue Jays

Park Name: Rogers Centre
Address: One Blue Jays Way, Toronto, Ontario, Canada
Capacity: 49,539

Opening Day: June 5, 1989
Dimensions (feet):
Left Field- 328
Center Field- 400
Right Field- 328
Cheapest seat: $11
Most Expensive seat: $210
Stadium Tours: The Rogers Centre Tour Experience is one hour in length. It's fully guided, goes behind the scenes and begins at the base of the CN Tower at Gate 3. Tours run hourly from June through October from 10am until 4pm. Cost: $16 for adults and $10-$12 for kids. Contact the tour office at 416-341-2770.

Some interesting information about the Rogers Centre:

❖ The Rogers Centre was the first stadium in the world with a retractable roof, allowing any sport to be played indoors or outdoors. Opening or closing the roof only takes 20 minutes and runs up an estimated $500 in utility bill. It moves at a rate of 70 feet per minute.

❖ The Jumbotron scoreboard in center field is 33-feet by 115-feet and has 67,200 light bulbs. It's one of the largest in the North America. It takes a crew of twenty to operate it.

❖ A 348 room hotel is located in center field. Seventy of those rooms have views of the field. On at least three occasions, spectators have been provided "auxiliary" entertainment by patrons inside the hotel during a game.

❖ When the roof is open, which is most of the time, the closed end of the stadium serves as a wind scoop that causes a downdraft in the outfield. This tends to prevent home runs.

◈ In 1992, this stadium set the World Record for the greatest number of Hot Air Balloons in an enclosed area: There were 46 inflated hot air balloons on the field.

◈ There are no bleachers at Rogers Centre. It's the only stadium in MLB able to make that claim.

◈ There are eight miles of zippers that connect the artificial turf that makes up the playing field at Rogers Centre.

◈ As far as we know, the Blue Jays are the only team in Major League Baseball to have never retired a player's number (other than Jackie Robinson, whose number is retired in every MLB stadium). They have no members in the Baseball Hall of Fame. While some former Blue Jays are in the Hall of Fame, none were inducted as Blue Jays.

Detroit
Things to do in Detroit:

Motown Historical Museum: The museum traces the roots of Motown's remarkable story and chronicles its impact on 20th century popular culture and musical styles. Follow the genesis of this company from the beginning when Berry Gordy, Jr. called his small house Hitsville USA (it's now home to the Motown Historical Museum). Follow the growth of Motown as it evolved into a major entertainment enterprise. The exhibits include a fascinating collection of historical photographs, artwork, music, costumes and other memorabilia from this booming musical era. Take a step back in time as you walk through the fully restored apartment that was once home to Berry Gordy, Jr, and stand in "Studio A", where Motown's greatest hits were recorded. Admission: $10 for adults and $8 for kids. For more information: http://www.motownmuseum.com

The Henry Ford Museum: Check out the actual seat in which Lincoln sat that fateful night in Ford Theatre, the original camp bed in which Washington slept, a tube containing the last breath taken by Thomas Edison, the limousine in which Kennedy rode on the day of his assassination, the bus in which Rosa Parks refused to give up her seat and so much more. It's impossible not to feel a sense of awe in this remarkable museum. This was one of the most memorable days we spent together over our seven year journey. You'll need a car to get to Dearborn, but it's worth the drive! Admission is $15 for adults and $11 for kids. For more information: www.hfmgv.org

Detroit Tigers

Park Name: Comerica Park
Address: 2100 Woodward Avenue, Detroit, MI 48201
Capacity: 40,950
Opening Day: April 11, 2000
Dimensions (feet):
Left Field- 346
Center Field- 402
Right Field- 330
Cheapest seat: $5
Most Expensive seat: $70
Stadium Tours: Public tours run from June - September, on Tuesdays and Fridays (non-game/non-event days), at 10 am, 12 pm, and 2 pm. Tour tickets are available at the Comerica Park Box Office located on Witherell Street the day of the tour. Advance ticket purchases are not required. Prices: $6 for adults and $3 for kids ages 4-14. For more information call (313) 471-2074.

Some interesting information about Comerica Park:

◈ Here's something you won't find in other ballparks: In the middle of the food court, there is a Ferris wheel with baseballs as cars and a merry-go-round with tigers instead of horses.

◈ Whenever the Tigers hit a home run, the eyes on the tiger statues on the top of the left field scoreboard light up and tiger growling is played through the public address system as the fountain in centerfield shoots water in the air.

◈ Don't miss the 13 foot high statues in Center Field that honor the Detroit Tigers' best players. Included are Willie Horton, Ty Cobb, Hank Greenberg, Charlie Gehringer, Hal Newhouser and Al Kaline. Each player's retired number appears below his statue. You should note, however, that Cobb has no retired number above his name - that is because he played before numbers were issued to the players.

◈ Baseball purists initially complained that Comerica Park's playing dimensions were too large and made it overly difficult to hit home runs. To remedy this, left-center fence was moved in from an original distance of 395 feet to 370 feet. Despite this move, Comerica's dimensions remain among of the largest in all of Major League Baseball, and some argue that further reductions in fence distance are needed.

◈ Look around and you'll notice the tiger motif in pretty much every element of the park. The most impressive are the stone sculptures of Tigers that flank every gate. The main gate is certainly one of the most impressive in all of baseball, with a number of large tiger sculptures adorned with bats and balls. No matter where you enter the ballpark, your first glimpse of Comerica Park will most likely include its all-brick exterior, which is circled by 33 stone tiger heads that have lighted baseballs between clinched teeth.

◈ Comerica is located near several downtown churches, including St. John's Episcopal Church and Central United Methodist Church. On the roof of St. John's is a banner that says "Pray Here for the Lions and Tigers!"

◈ Comerica Park might be best known for its towering upper deck structures, but it has no upper deck seating, providing fans an unobstructed view of the field and the downtown skyline.

⬦ As for the ballpark fare, there are a number of Little Caeser's pizza stands throughout the ballpark, which is no surprise since the Tigers' owner made his millions by founding the chain.

⬦ During night games it's not uncommon for large flocks of seagulls to frolic in the outfield grass.

⬦ The field itself features a distinctive dirt strip between home plate and the pitcher's mound. This strip, sometimes known as the "keyhole", was common in early ballparks, yet very rare in modern facilities. The only other stadium with such a feature is Chase Field, home of the Arizona Diamondbacks.

⬦ After Friday and Saturday games, there is an on-field fireworks display for the fans to enjoy.

⬦ Take some time before the game to walk around the entire main concourse. You can take in the Tigers' Walk of Fame, with its historical elements and memorabilia celebrating the Tigers' rich history. The Walk of Fame is punctuated by six large "decade bats" that denote each era in Tigers' baseball with artifacts, photos and display cases. It's pretty cool.

⬦ During an episode of *This Week In Baseball* in 1999, the host of the show and a lucky fan came to the park to throw a baseball that was signed by the entire 1999 Tigers team into the dirt that was being dug up to make the home plate area at Comerica Park. The ball is treated as a time capsule and when Comerica Park is demolished in the distant future, the workers will be able to find the ball.

⬦ Comerica Park includes eight surrounding buildings that house restaurants, cool shops and entertainment options that create a mini city within a city.

Cleveland
Things to do in Cleveland:

Rock and Roll Hall of Fame and Museum: This is the preeminent home for the celebration and study of rock and roll music. With a dizzying array of exhibits filled with painstakingly preserved and creatively displayed artifacts, this is the ultimate venue for learning about rock and roll and how it continues to shape our lives. Just like the music to which it pays homage, the Rock Hall exudes coolness. From the adventurously wide-open architecture and compellingly eye-popping displays to the sing-along soundtrack of continuously streaming rock and roll hits, this is one museum experience that really rocks. Admission is $22 for adults and $13 for kids. For more information: www.rockhall.com

Great Lakes Science Center: Located on the shores of Lake Erie next to the Rock and Roll Hall of Fame, this is one of America's largest interactive science museums. More than 400 hands-on exhibits, larger-than-life OMNIMAX films, and live demonstrations make the Science Center a terrific experience. Perfect for kids 6-16 years. Admission is under $10. For more information: www.greatscience.com

Cleveland Indians

Park Name: Progressive Field (it was called Jacobs Field when we visited the park)
Address: 2401 Ontario Street, Cleveland, OH 44115
Capacity: 43,345
Opening Day: April 4, 1994
Dimensions (feet):
Left Field- 325
Center Field- 405

Right Field- 325
Cheapest seat: $7
Most Expensive seat: $100
Stadium Tours: A tour at Progressive Field will provide the opportunity to visit the batting cages, bullpen, press box, dugout, and Heritage Park. Tours are given from May through September. Tickets are available at Indians Team Shop locations, by phone at 216.420.HITS and online at Indians.com. Ticket prices are $7.50 for adults and $5.50 for kids. Tour times vary.

Some interesting information about Progressive Field:

◈ The seats at Progressive Field down both lines are angled towards home plate so that fans don't need to turn their heads to watch the game. Nice touch!

◈ The bullpens are elevated 4 feet 6 inches above the playing field to allow the fans to see who is warming up.

◈ Jacobs Field set a major league record between June 12, 1995 and April 4, 2001 by selling out 455 straight games. Demand for tickets was so great that all 81 home games were sold out before opening day on three separate occasions. The Indians "retired" the number 455 in honor of the sellout record. The Boston Red Sox later surpassed this record, when Fenway Park recorded 456 straight sellouts on September 9, 2008.

◈ The Indians' mascot, Slider, is one of only three Major League Baseball team mascots to be inducted into the Mascot Hall of Fame (bet you didn't even know there was a HOF for mascots!).

◈ The original Home plate from Cleveland Municipal Stadium was transplanted to Progressive Field at end of 1993 season.

◈ You can't miss the scoreboard above the bleachers in right field. It is one of the largest freestanding scoreboards in baseball, measuring 120 feet tall and 222 feet wide.

◈ It is rumored that small time Chicago mobster Karl Klessig, who disappeared many years ago when he attempted to expand his operations into Cleveland, is buried under what is now Progressive Field. Known for his questionable hygiene (he eschewed frequent bathing), it is more than a bit ironic that millions of gnats have interrupted games played in that park over the years.

Pittsburgh
Things to do in Pittsburgh:

Duquesne Incline: Scale Mount Washington in one of two original 1877 cable cars for a fun and unique ride and a breathtaking view of the Pittsburgh skyline when you reach the top of the 400-foot incline. It's a very memorable experience that you may want to take near mealtime as there are a number of restaurants at the top. For more information: http://incline.pghfree.net/

Sandcastle Water Park: Enjoy fourteen twisting, turning, plunging, and churning waterslides. There are pools for adults (including the world's biggest hot tub) and pools for kids (including Wet Willie's Water Works). Surrounding it all is the Lazy River, a gently flowing stream where you can float on a tube for hours. There's also a 20,000-square-foot wave pool and a quarter-mile go-kart track. For more information: www.sandcastlewaterpark.com

Pro Football Hall of Fame: We know...it's not in Pittsburgh. But if you find yourself driving between Pittsburgh or Cleveland and Cincinnati, you'll want to stop in Canton, Ohio to visit this shrine to the 'other' national sport. A truly exhilarating museum and exhibition center, the Pro Football Hall of Fame pays tribute to the talents and triumphs of pro football's greatest stars. Chronicled within the walls of the Hall of Fame are the stories and circumstances of play that bring to life words such as courage, dedication, vision, fair play, and skill. And we dare you to get out of the gift shop unscathed! For more information: www.profootballhof.com

Pittsburgh Pirates

Park Name: PNC Park
Address: 115 Federal Street, Pittsburgh, PA 15212
Capacity: 38,362
Opening Day: April 9, 2001
Dimensions (feet):
Left Field- 325
Center Field- 399
Right Field- 320
Cheapest seat: $9
Most Expensive seat: $210
Stadium Tours: This is a fairly comprehensive tour that includes the Pirates dugout & warning track, batting cages, Pittsburgh Baseball Club Level, press box, Tour Theatre & Museum, and Hall of Fame Club. The tour lasts approximately 90 minutes. Tours are wheelchair and stroller accessible. All tours begin at the Willie Stargell Statue Gate (located on Federal Street). Cost: $7 for adults and $5 for kids.

Some interesting information about PNC Park:

◈ PNC Park is the first ballpark with a two-deck design to be built since Milwaukee's County Stadium was completed in 1953. Because of its intimate design, the highest seat is just 88 feet from the field, giving every fan in the park an ideal sight line.

◈ Designed to fit within the existing city grid, PNC Park is orientated to allow a great majority of spectators a spectacular view of the Clemente Bridge and the downtown skyline beyond. With a capacity of 38,362, PNC Park is baseball's second smallest ballpark.

◈ For a few bucks, you can take a ferry to the ballpark, or you can park at the nearby city garage and walk across the Roberto Clemente bridge, the focal eye candy from inside the ballpark.

◈ Statues of Honus Wagner, Willie Stargell and Roberto Clemente are also outside the ballpark. Wagner's statue was originally unveiled at The Pirates' former home, Forbes Field, in 1955. The base of Clemente's statue is shaped like a baseball diamond, with dirt from three of the fields Clemente played at—Santurce Field in Puerto Rico, Forbes Field, and Three Rivers Stadium—at each base. On October 1, 2000, after the final game at Three Rivers Stadium, Stargell threw out the ceremonial last pitch. He was presented with a model of a statue that was to be erected in his honor outside of PNC Park but he never saw the actual statue. It was officially unveiled on April 7, 2001, however, Stargell could not attend due to health problems and died of a stroke two days later.

◈ An out of town scoreboard is part of the 21 foot high right field fence, in honor of Pirates legend Roberto Clemente, one of the greatest right fielders in baseball history, who wore number 21.

◈ When you're in Philly, you need to eat the Philly Cheese Steak. When in Milwaukee, you gotta down a bratwurst. And when you're at PNC Park, you need to head directly over to the world famous Primanti Brothers. Their famous steak sandwich, with fries and coleslaw piled between two slices of Italian bread is as good as it gets. They have concessions on each level.

◈ This is a stadium that is designed to reward visitors who choose to sit in the top deck. You can take it all in as you enjoy views of Mt. Washington, numerous bridges and skyscrapers, including the glass castle PPG structure, and the occasional boat chugging along the river. Like San Francisco's AT&T Park, the worse the seat, the better the view.

◈ The Pirates copied Milwaukee's famous Sausage Race, by racing costumed pierogis (dumplings filled with cottage cheese, potato, or sauerkraut) between the fifth and sixth innings.

◈ Bullpens are on the field like they were at Forbes Field, where the Pirates played for 61 years. The only other field currently set up this way is Wrigley Field, home of the Cubs.

◈ Former Pirate great Manny Sanguillen actually owns and operates a barbeque in the outfield bleachers, and will sign autographs while you wait for your order.

◈ To hit a ball into the Alleghany River, running behind right center field, you'd have to hit it at least 443 feet and 4 inches. It has only been done once during an actual game: Daryle Ward, of the Houston Astros, dinged one into the river in 2002.

Cincinnati
Things to do in Cincinnati:

Cincinnati Reds Hall of Fame and Museum: The Cincinnati Reds have a storied history: They were the first professional club, hosted the first night game, and dominated the 1970s with the "Big Red Machine". The Cincinnati Reds Hall of Fame and Museum covers all facets of the team's history. There are several exhibits geared toward children, such as a pitching mound, an interactive radio booth, and a clubhouse that allows kids to dress up like their favorite players. The tour concludes in the plaque room with all inductees of the team's hall of fame (there's a blank spot on the wall that pays homage of Pete Rose, who has been banned from all baseball honors). Be sure to show up a few hours before game time to take in this special place since it's located contiguously to the ballpark. Admission: $10 for adults and $8 for kids. For more information: http://cincinnati.reds.mlb.com/cin/ballpark/museum/hours.jsp

The National Underground Railroad Freedom Center: Around 1800, an informal network of "safe houses," "conductors" and "abolitionists" began to actively resist the enslavement of African Americans in the South. This network eventually became known as the Underground Railroad. The National Underground Railroad Freedom Center is located on the banks of the Ohio River—the historic dividing line between North and South. The Center honors this major Underground Railroad crossing point and illuminates the stories of individuals who helped support the courageous acts of self liberation of those who escaped from slavery. Certainly warrants a visit if you have the time. For more information: http://www.freedomcenter.org/

Cincinnati Zoo and Botanical Garden: This is the second oldest zoo in the U.S. and considered to be one of the best. It is most renowned for its endangered species and birthing programs, particularly for gorillas and white tigers. There is also a wonderful collection of felines and a great manatee exhibit. For more information, go to www.cincinnatizoo.org

Cincinnati Reds

Park Name: Great American Ballpark
Address: 100 Joe Nuxhall Way, Cincinnati, Ohio 45202
Capacity: 42,271
Opening Day: March 31, 2003
Dimensions (feet):
Left Field- 328
Center Field- 404
Right Field- 325
Cheapest seat: $5
Most Expensive seat: $230
Stadium Tours: There are stadium tours during the season, but only for night games. You'll want to allow two and a half hours for the tour. The guided portion of the ballpark tour averages 90 minutes in duration. The self-guided Reds Hall of Fame tour is 45-60 minutes (and is so engrossing, you may want to leave even more time). The cost of the tour is $15 for adults and $13 for kids, and this includes admission into the Reds. Tickets can also be purchased at the Reds Hall of Fame Box Office, located on the west side (Joe Nuxhall Way) of Great American Ball Park or on the Reds website.

Some interesting information about Great American Ballpark:

❖ Contrary to popular belief, the park's name is not a patriotic reference. As with many ballparks, ownership added to its coffers by bringing in a business sponsor. In this case, it's the Great American Insurance Group.

❖ Great American Ballpark pays tribute to former Reds' homes. Take a look at the scoreboard clock in left field... it's a replica of the one that sat in Crosley Field (the Reds' home from 1912-1970). The main entry and seats were designed to resemble the old park.

❖ Check out the rose garden outside the stadium. It's planted on the very spot where Pete Rose's record 4192nd base hit landed in old Riverfront Stadium (upon which Great American Ballpark is built). On a separate note, if you're into history, it's said that second base occupies the spot where the home of Roy Rogers, the singing cowboy, once stood.

❖ The architects put quite a bit of thought into designing a 35' wide break in the stands between home plate and third base, called "The Gap". It provides views into the stadium from downtown and out to the skyline from within the park.

❖ If your budget allows, this is a good stadium to consider buying the best seats. Some are located just 50 feet from home plate (you'll actually be closer to the batter than the pitcher, who stands over 60 feet away). And these babies are padded. The high price does include free grub, just in case you need a reason to justify the expense.

❖ This is important. We ate the hot dogs in all thirty stadiums. Every damn one! The Skyline Chili Dogs served at

Great American Ballpark were the finest we had. There wasn't even a close second place. Boiled in beer and then placed on a fresh bun, they are lathered in Skyline Chili and finely grated cheddar cheese. The cheese completely melts before you hit your seat. Messy? You betcha. Heavenly? Worth dying for! They are served at Skyline concessions throughout the park.

❖ Not much is mentioned in this book about shopping inside the stadiums. That's because most are merchandised with predictable lines of apparel, nick-knacks, baseballs, etc. However, the Reds main store offers up real game-used bats and jerseys. There is also quite a bit of retro apparel, including a Johnnie Bench jersey that my son would have killed for but whose father was far too frugal. It may be the best team store in the majors and you'll want to leave enough time to check it out.

❖ As you walk around the perimeter of the stadium, you'll hit Crosley Terrace at the intersection of Second and Main Streets. Most fans actually pass through this area before entering the ballpark. The terrace features statues of Crosley Field-era players (Joe Nuxhall, Ernie Lombardi, Ted Kluszewski and Frank Robinson).

❖ If your group is all of drinking age (or has credible fake ID's), a brewpub, known as the Machine Room, is located near the Reds bullpen. It's a terrific place to catch the ballgame. Not coincidentally, the bar features tons of memorabilia from the Big Red Machine era.

❖ When you look into right center field, you'll see two smokestacks, reminiscent of the steamboats that were common on the Ohio River over a century ago. They serve a purpose beyond their historical reference. When the Reds strike out a batter, smoke blows out of the stacks. Fireworks are launched from the stacks after every Reds home run and win.

◈ A mosaic paying tribute to two legendary Reds teams: the 1869 Red Stockings, Major League Baseball's first professional team, and the 1975 Big Red Machine club that won the first of two consecutive World Series, are just inside the main entrance.

◈ Fix your eyes into right field. You'll see a "Hit Me" sign located between the Power Stacks. If a player hits the sign, a randomly selected fan will win the Toyota pickup truck located on top of an elevator shaft approximately 500 feet from home plate beyond the center field fence. This will give you one more thing to cheer for when the big hitters bring their lumber up to the plate.

◈ Perhaps the most unique, but hidden feature of this stadium is the string of quotes that wrap around the interior of the club level concourse, visible from the wide concourse behind the third base grandstand. Don't miss it... every great baseball quote can be found if you're willing to take the time to look at them. Among our favorites are Casey Stengel's "I don't like them fellas who drive in two runs and let in three." Then there is Pete Rose's quote: "I'd walk through Hell in a gasoline suit to play baseball."

◈ We don't want to spook you, but the base paths have allegedly been filled with dirt from a local graveyard. So don't be surprised if you see some crazy bounces.

◈ A circle in left-center marked "4,192" commemorates Pete Rose's 4,192nd hit on September 10, 1985, which broke Ty Cobb's career hits record.

East Coast Cities and Stadiums
Washington D.C.
Things to do in Washington D.C.:

Bike and Roll Bicycle Rentals: Since cars aren't allowed on the Mall and walking takes up quite a bit of time, a bike rental provides the perfect way to catch the sites. We grabbed a map of the city and visited the Mall and all its memorials, rode to the White House and Smithsonian Museum (see more about this below) before returning our transports. Bike The Sites also offers guided tours of the city. Plan to spend about $35 per person for the rentals. You'll have a ball!! More information at: http://www.bikethesites.com/rentals.htm.

City Segway Tours of Washington DC: Here's another great way to tour the nation's Capital. As you may already know, the Segway is a self-balancing, personal transportation device that's designed to operate in any pedestrian environment. As you cruise through the Nation's Capital, past the monuments, White House, Supreme Court, Ford Theatre, and Smithsonian Museums, you will receive heaps of information and fantastic photo ops. There is a 30 minute orientation prior to the tour. Riders must be 16 years or older and weigh at least 100 pounds. $70 per person. For more information: http://citysegwaytours.com/washington-dc

National Air and Space Museum: The most popular of the Smithsonian museums features the actual Wright Brothers' 1903 Flyer, Lindbergh's Spirit of St. Louis and the Apollo 11 command module. In fact, this museum maintains the largest collection of historic air and spacecraft in the world. This is probably the most interesting of the Smithsonian's museums (there are 19 of them plus the National Zoo) for people of all ages. For more information: http://www.nasm.si.edu

Arlington National Cemetery: A cemetery is not generally an interesting place to take kids, but this is really special. There are over 300,000 veterans from every American war buried among the 200 acres. Plan on spending at least two hours during your visit and pay your respects to the many special people interred here, including the Tomb of the Unknown Soldier (stay for the changing of the guards presentation...it'll bring tears!) and the Kennedy grave site with its eternal flame. Be sure to check out the gravestone of former heavyweight champion Joe Louis. Arlington National Cemetery is an easy subway ride from the city. For more information: http://www.arlingtoncemetery.org

U.S. Capital Tour: We received a tour reservation through our U.S. Representative's office. Doing so allowed us to avoid the large crowds and provided easier access. We traveled through the tunnels between the office building and the Capitol. You get to see an introductory movie, the dome, statues, whispering spot, etc. You also get to sit in the gallery and watch Senators orate on whatever business is before them (if they're in session at the time). It's very cool. Be sure to contact your U.S. Representative or Senator's office for information and tickets. Along the same lines, if you can use your political influence to secure personal tours of the White House and/or Supreme Court, go for it.

Washington Nationals

Park Name: Nationals Park
Address: 1500 South Capitol Street, SE, Washington, DC 20003
Capacity: 41,546
Opening Day: March 30, 2008
Dimensions (feet):

Left Field- 336 feet
Center Field- 402 feet
Right Field- 335 feet
Cheapest seat: $5
Most Expensive seat: $325
Stadium Tours: The Nationals offer a 10:30 a.m. game-day tour of the park when they have a night game at home. Over the course of an hour, guides will take you to The PNC Diamond Club, the Lexus Presidents Club, the Stars & Stripes Club, The Press Box, The Shirley Povich Media Center (named for the legendary Washington sports journalist, you can see the typewriter used by Povich, who worked in the press box for 75 years), and the visiting team dugout. Cost: $15 for adults and $10 for kids. You can buy tickets online at the team's website (washington.nationals.mlb.com), at the stadium kiosks located at the Center Field Gate next to the team store, or at the Box Office.

Some interesting information about Nationals Park:

◈ Fans entering through the outfield gates never get to see the ballpark's futuristic looking façade. And that's a big mistake. You need to venture over to the Home Plate gate and you'll see a façade made from steel, glass and pre-cast concrete that is dramatic, beautiful and unlike any other ballpark.

◈ Be sure to walk around the concourses and seating decks at Nationals Park because you'll be treated to a visual tour of Washington D.C. They are configured to create a variety of distinct neighborhoods. As you cruise around the vertical circulation ramps throughout the various levels of the ballpark, you'll see panoramic views of the riverfront, Navy Yard, the surrounding city and landmarks such as the Capitol and the Washington Monument.

◈ Inspiration for the look of the ballpark is taken from the East Wing of the National Gallery of Art, designed by world famous architect I.M. Pei.

◈ Notice the odd right-angled jog into the right-center field fence? It is a replica of the fence at the now demolished Griffith Stadium, the former home of the Washington Senators.

◈ Washington Nationals Park would not be complete without some cherry trees. Fourteen Kwanzan Japanese cherry trees are located behind the left field stands, in the center field plaza and left field concourse. You won't see these trees in any other ballpark.

◈ See if you can find the three statues honoring Walter Johnson of the original Washington Senators, Frank Howard, and Josh Gibson of the old Negro League Homestead Grays, which played many of its games in Washington.

◈ There's a chance to make your own Screech Mascot at the ballpark's special make your own mascot store. It's located in the Center Field section of the park as part of the Build a Bear Store.

◈ Nationals Park is actually the first LEEDS-certified green major professional sports stadium in the US.

◈ If you stroll to your seats in the lower level, be sure to check out the concrete support columns that are adorned by 10-foot Arthur Miller paintings of Hall of

Famers, both from Washington and around the league. On the wall of the concourse behind home plate are lighted timelines that examine Washington's baseball history.

❖ The Nationals pay homage to the history of baseball in Washington DC. If you can get inside the PNC Diamond Club, you'll have a chance to see the actual seat from RFK Stadium that was painted white to commemorate a mammoth homer hit by Frank Howard. It was the only white seat in the entire stadium and is quite famous among the locals. Head over to the bar at the PNC Diamond Club and you can see a replica scoreboard with the line score from Game 7 of the 1924 World Series. It displays a 4-3 victory in 12 innings by the Senators over the New York Giants. What's the big deal? That win at Griffith Stadium secured Washington's only World Series championship. Ever. They are due for another one…but only after the Cubs pick up their first World Series since 1908.

❖ Don't take a bathroom break during the middle the 4th inning at this stadium. That's when the Racing Presidents make their appearance. The race features the four presidents immortalized on Mount Rushmore - George Washington, Thomas Jefferson, Abraham Lincoln and Teddy Roosevelt. Standing about ten feet tall, the oversized foam caricature heads take off from center field and race along the warning track until they reach the Nationals' dugout. Sadly, Teddy Roosevelt has yet to win. Fans have taken to chanting "Let Teddy Win". And if you're really lucky and happen to be at a game that lasts at least 13 innings, the Racing Presidents go at it again.

Baltimore
Things to do in Baltimore:

Inner Harbor: One of America's oldest seaports, dating from the1600s, is an important landmark and popular tourist destination. Park your car and follow the brick promenade through this bustling complex of eateries, stores, museums, entertainment and children's attractions. Sample the fresh seafood right out of Chesapeake Bay. Don't miss the Sports Museum located next to Camden Yards or the USS Constitution, a restored Civil War sloop. For more information: http://baltimore.org/about-baltimore/inner-harbor

Fort McHenry National Monument: This is the historic fort that inspired Francis Scott Key to write the U.S. national anthem. If you like history, this is a must-see. View the short, informative film in the Visitor's Center. At the end of the movie, the drapes slowly open to a view of the American flag flying over the fort while the Star Spangled Banner is sung by the Naval Academy Choir. It's an extremely moving moment. There's a self guided tour of the fort and barracks. For more information: http://www.nps.gov/fomc/index.htm

National Aquarium: Conveniently located on the Inner Harbor, the National Aquarium may be the finest in the world. It offers remarkable exhibits and a great 4D IMAX show. Don't miss the Dolphin Show (catch the early one at 11am to avoid the crowd), Australia Exhibit and Sting Ray Feeding. It's reasonably priced (about $30 for adults and $20 for kids). For more information: www.aqua.org.

Babe Ruth Museum: This is the ultimate shrine to the Greatest of them All. The Sultan of Swat. The King of Clout.

The Great Bambino. It doesn't matter what you call him, you have to stop by his birthplace when you're in Baltimore. Not only will you see his original home, but you'll experience life at the turn of the 20th century. It's a long fly ball from Camden Yards, home of the Baltimore Orioles, so plan to get to the park an hour earlier and check this cool place out. It's cheap: $6 for adults and $4 for kids. If you have the time, pay a visit to the Sports Legend Museum next door at Camden Yards where you'll find exhibits on the Orioles, Ravens, Colts and other teams and athletes associated with the state of Maryland. For more information: http://www.baberuthmuseum.com/

Baltimore Orioles

Park Name: Oriole Park at Camden Yards
Address: 333 West Camden Street, Baltimore, MD 21201
Capacity: 48,876
Opening Day: April 6, 1992
Dimensions (feet):
Left Field- 333
Center Field- 410
Right Field- 318
Cheapest seat: $8 (standing room only)
Most Expensive seat: $55
Stadium Tours: The Orioles offer a 90 minute stadium tour that includes a visit to the Orioles dugout, the Press Box, the Scoreboard Control Room and more. There's also a historical perspective at Camden Yards that focuses on the old Railroad, the Inner Harbor and the city's most famous baseball player (Babe Ruth). Price: $6-$9 (call 410- 547-6234 to reserve a tour).

Some interesting information about Camden Yards:

◈ Camden Yards is two blocks from the birthplace of George Herman "Babe" Ruth (see prior page for more about this). In fact, Babe Ruth's adopted father (Jack Dunn) owned a tavern located where center field now sits!

◈ Don't even think of missing the Sports Legends Museum at Camden Yards. The museum has hundreds of biographical sketches and photographs of the more than 200 Maryland born or based athletes inducted into the Hall. Check out Jimmie Foxx's catchers' mask, Frank "Home Run" Baker's 1922 Yankee's sweater, and so much more. It's $8 for adults and $6 for kids. By the way, the museum store is pretty cool…where else are you going to find a John Unitas jersey and Babe Ruth Wall Ornament in the same place?

◈ Monday and Thursday is Oriole Alumni Autograph day and former players can be found on Eutaw Street, which is located between the field and warehouse beyond right field.

◈ Boog's BBQ is behind the Center Field Fence and former Oriole All Star Boog Powell can frequently be found signing autographs and serving up some good, old fashioned BBQ.

◈ A number of home run balls have landed on Eutaw Street, and the Orioles organization has marked the spots with small baseball-shaped bronze plaques embedded in the street itself.

◈ While every stadium features the numbers of its finest retired players, the uniforms of retired Orioles are displayed in cement sculptures near stadium entrances. It's a great place to take pictures.

❖ The song, *Thank God I'm a Country Boy,* is played during the seventh-inning stretch at every home game. Don't ask why a song written and sung by a John Denver, who hailed from Colorado, would become a standard in Baltimore. Just go with it!

❖ Every seat in Camden Yards is green except for two: An orange seat (located in Section 96, Row D, Seat 23 in the right-center field bleachers) commemorates the landing spot of Eddie Murray's 500th home run. A red seat (Section 86, Row FF, Seat 10 in the left field bleachers) was the landing spot for Cal Ripken Jr.'s 278th home run as a short stop, breaking Chicago Cubs legend Ernie Bank's record for the position.

❖ Camden Yards got its name because it was built on the site of the old B+O Railroad station at Camden. The old B+O Railroad warehouse stands alongside the stadium to this day. It happens to be the longest building on the East Coast (1016 feet long).

❖ Check out the aisle seats at Camden Yards. Each and every one features the Orioles logo from the 1890's.

❖ The ballpark features double deck bullpens in left-center field.

❖ Keep your eye on *The Sun* sign on the center field scoreboard or you'll miss the following: The "H" flashes when the scoring decision is a hit and the "E" flashes when it's an error.

❖ The foul poles at Camden Yards are the same ones used at Memorial Stadium, the former home of the Orioles.

Philadelphia
Things to do in Philadelphia:

Independence Hall: Consider what happened under one roof: It was in the Assembly Room of this building that George Washington was appointed Commander in Chief of the Continental Army in 1775 and the Declaration of Independence was adopted on July 4, 1776. In the same room the design of the American flag was agreed upon in 1777, the Articles of Confederation were adopted in 1781, and the U. S. Constitution was drafted in 1787. Visitors are admitted for free, but you need to secure a timed tour ticket. Make your high school American History teacher proud and pay Independence Hall a visit. For more information: http://www.nps.gov/inde/independence-hall-1.htm

Liberty Bell: The actual Liberty Bell is displayed in a magnificent glass chamber with Independence Hall in the background. Here's an opportunity to get within inches of one of the greatest icons of American history. Here's a bit of trivia: The Liberty Bell weighs 2000 lbs. and hangs from its original American elm oak yoke. For more information: http://www.nps.gov/inde/liberty-bell-center.htm

U.S. Mint: Would you like to actually watch money being made? Then you have to visit the Philadelphia Mint. You can take a free 45 minute self-guided tour and check out the huge equipment that works 24 hours a day, five days a week making our coin currency. There is an amazing amount of craftsmanship that goes into the various stages of the minting process, from the original designs and sculptures to the actual striking of the coins. You'll see it all! The United States Mint at Philadelphia is open for public tours Monday through Friday from 9 am to 3 pm; no reservations are necessary. As an aside, there is a cemetery across the street from the U.S.

Mint that houses the gravesite of none other than Benjamin Franklin. It's worth strolling over for a look. For more information about the Mint: http://www.usmint.gov/about_the_mint/mint_facilities/index.cfm?action=PA_facilities

Philly Cheesesteak Sandwich: You simply cannot go to Philadelphia without sampling this city's prized cuisine! There are a number of things you need to consider in your search for the perfect cheesesteak. A proper Philly cheesesteak is made with real beef – fresh, not frozen. It is cooked on a grill using grease. As it is cooked, it should be chopped to bits. You then choose which cheese you prefer (Cheez Whiz is a sure winner, by the way) and whether you want onions, peppers or other toppings. When the sandwich is served, the juices should drip from your sandwich. In order to avoid ruining their clothes, locals have learned the "Philadelphia Lean", comprised of bending forward to eat the cheesesteak, to avoid staining their clothing. There are several places that offer up fresh made, mouth-watering Philly Cheesesteak sandwiches. There's Pagano's Steaks at 920 W Girard Ave. But the real debate among insiders is whether Pat's or Gino's is the best. Cheesesteaks were invented in the 1930's at Pat's Steaks, located in the heart of South Philadelphia, hence the addition of "Philly" to the name. Jim's Steaks, at 4th and South Street, has been in business for over 60 years, and is a favorite of many locals. We'll let you make the call on this one.

Eastern State Penitentiary: The Eastern State Penitentiary Historic Site was once the most famous and expensive prison in the world, but stands today in ruin, a haunting world of crumbling cellblocks and empty guard towers. Known for its grand architecture and strict discipline, this was the world's first true "penitentiary," a prison designed to inspire penitence, or true regret, in the hearts of convicts.

Tours today include the cellblocks, solitary punishment cells, Al Capone's Cell, and Death Row. Cost: $12 for adults and $8 for kids. More information: http://easternstate.org/

Philadelphia Phillies

Park Name: Citizens Bank Park
Address: Pattison Avenue, Philadelphia, PA
Capacity: 43,647
Opening Day: April 12, 2004
Dimensions (feet):
Left Field- 329
Center Field- 401
Right Field- 330
Cheapest seat: $20
Most Expensive seat: $60
Stadium Tours: After a brief audio-visual presentation of the park, your tour will include the Phillies dugout, Diamond Club (which features the glass-enclosed batting cages), and the Hall of Fame Club. Tours last approximately 90 minutes and start and end at the Clubhouse Store. On Monday through Saturday game days, tours are offered at 10:30am and 12:30pm. There are no tours on Sundays. You can reserve your tour at the Phillies' website or by calling 215-463-1000. Reservations are required. Cost: $6 for kids, $10 for adults.

Some interesting information about Citizens Bank Park:

◇ We're going to take the ballpark's word on this one, but there are allegedly 450,000 hand laid bricks that make up the walls around Citizens Bank Park.

◈ You can't help but notice the gigantic Neon Liberty Bell located in right-center field above the rooftop bleacher seats. It towers 102 feet above street level, and whenever a Phillies player hits a home run, the bell rings and rocks the entire stadium.

◈ The other striking feature in this ballpark is the gigantic scoreboard. It's the largest LED screen in the National League, taking up 2,759 square feet. It's loaded with information and we found it to be the most informative and intuitive one in baseball. Trust me, you'll be well informed of the goings on in Philly and elsewhere in baseball when you stay tuned to this bad boy.

◈ Get to Citizens Bank Park early and spend some time at Ashburn's Alley. This area was named after Phillies Hall of Fame center fielder Richie Ashburn, who played for the team from 1948 to 1959 and was a Phillies broadcaster from 1963 until his death in 1997. Located in the outfield concourse, Ashburn's Alley features a street-fair type atmosphere, picnic areas, a walk through Phillies' Memory Lane, and a great Philadelphia-themed concession area that will tax your aorta but please your taste buds (give the cheesesteaks and hoagies a try if you don't believe me). The best place for a meal in Ashburn's Alley is Bull's BBQ, where pulled barbecue pork, ribs and turkey are served by Bull himself – former Phillies slugger Greg Luzinski -who signs autographs as well. Ashburn Alley opens two and a half hours before game time.

◈ As you walk around the inside of the stadium, you'll find 10-foot tall bronze sculptures of Phillies legends Steve Carlton, Richie Ashburn, Mike Schmidt, and Robin Roberts.

◈ Talk about a ballpark designed to give a competitive advantage to the home team. The bi-level bullpens located in right-center field allow fans to get very close to the visiting team's pitchers, who sit in the top level. And get this: Fans are allowed to heckle the opposing pitchers, but must keep it clean.

◈ If the starting lineup is important to you, be sure to enter via the left field gate, where you'll find The Phillies starting lineup blown up on giant 10-foot-tall by 5-foot-wide baseball cards.

◈ No Phillies game is complete without witnessing the genius that is the Phillie Phanatic. Because he only makes one on-field appearance during the game, remember to stay in your seat for the 6th inning. He offers up the best mascot performance in baseball.

New York City
Things to do in New York City:

Central Park: Just walk in at 59th Street and wander around. Head over to the zoo. Check out the Dairy, which is now the spot for shopping. Ride the carousel. Stop by Strawberry Fields at 72nd Street to see The Dakota (John Lennon's former apartment). You can take a horse-drawn carriage ride or ride a horse yourself. Have lunch at the Boathouse or just buy food from one of the many vending carts. And if you want a more comprehensive look at Central Park, try Central Park Bike Tours. You'll get a two hour guided tour of the big Oasis that's full of visual and factual information. You can contact the touring company at: biketours1@aol.com.

Statue of Liberty and Ellis Island: Line up at Battery Park and catch the ferry to the Statue of Liberty. If you want to go inside the base of the Statue of Liberty museum, you must make a reservation. Just remember, if you want to go to the highest allowable point, you will have to travel up one hundred seventy one stairs and then back down. For reservations and more information: http://www.nps.gov/stli/planyourvisit/feesandreservations.htm. When you're finished with Lady Liberty, you'll catch another ferry to Ellis Island. The ferries run regularly. Definitely do the audio tour at Ellis Island. You'll become completely immersed in the émigré experience as you hear and read the stories of the immigrants and the families they left behind for a better life. If your family emigrated from Europe between 1892 and 1954, you can trace their arrival in the library at Ellis Island. Allow at least a half day for these two experiences. For more information on Ellis Island: http://www.ellisisland.org/

Empire State Building: The Empire State Building, a New York City landmark, soars more than a quarter of a mile into the sky above the heart of Manhattan. While we didn't spot King Kong, Tom Hanks or Meg Ryan (remember the scene from *Sleepless in Seattle?*), we did enjoy the Observatory located on the 86th floor, 1,050 feet above the city's bustling streets. It offers panoramic views of New York City from within a glass enclosed pavilion and from the surrounding open-air promenade. Buy tickets the day of your visit for about $15 each. Get there early to beat the crowds. For more information: http://www.esbnyc.com

Hayden Planetarium (part of the American Museum of Natural History): No need to settle for just looking at the stars - this $210 million planetarium is a virtual joyride through the universe. It feels real and is quite effective at giving anyone a deeper understanding of our place in the universe. Admission is free with tickets to the museum: $8.50 for kids and $15 for adults (by the way, the rest of the museum isn't too shabby either...you did see *Night at the Museum*, didn't you?). For more information: http://www.amnh.org/rose/

New York Yankees

Park Name: New Yankee Stadium
Address: One East 161st Street, Bronx, NY 01451
Capacity: 52,325
First Official Game: April 16, 2009
Dimensions (feet):
Left Field- 318
Center Field- 408
Right Field- 314
Cheapest seat: $14(upper bleachers)
Most Expensive game day seat: $300

Stadium Tours: All tour tickets are sold on a first-come, first-served basis and are subject to availability. The Classic Tour costs $20 per person during the season. It lasts 45 minutes to one hour and includes visits to the New York Yankees Museum, Monument Park, the dugout and clubhouse/batting cage area. Classic Tours for individuals (from 1-11 people) begin every 20 minutes from 12:00pm - 1:40 pm. Tickets may be purchased over the phone in advance of 10 days from the tour date via Ticketmaster at 1-877-469-9849 and at any Ticketmaster or Yankees Clubhouse Shop.

Some interesting information about Yankee Stadium:

◈ The New Yankee Stadium cost an estimated $1.3 Billion to build. By comparison, the Old Yankee Stadium cost $2.5 Million to build in the early 1920's.

◈ In Yankee Stadium's Monument Park, there are 20 plaques and six standing monuments honoring the Yankees' most revered legends. The monuments honor Miller Huggins (the Manager who guided the Yankees to 3 World Series and 6 American League pennants in the 1920's), Babe Ruth, Lou Gehrig, Joe DiMaggio, Mickey Mantle and the victims of the 9/11 attacks.

◈ The New Yankee Stadium features an abundance of over the top, artery clogging foods from wonderful providers such as Johnny Rockets, Brother Jimmy's BBQ (don't even think of missing the Frickles…aka: deep fried pickles), Lobel's Deli (with its fresh carved meat sandwiches), and Carl's Philly Cheesesteak. Yankee Stadium is the only ballpark, as far as we know, that sells both Nathan's and Hebrew National hot dogs. Feel free to wash down these goodies with some Carvel's Ice Cream. Oh, if you want something a bit more healthy, there is a sushi bar for the three fans who desire raw fish at a ballgame.

◈ The signature copper frieze, the lattice work that once rimmed the original Yankee Stadium roof, is replicated in its identical location at the new stadium.

◈ The new stadium has the exact same field dimensions and bullpen placements as the old Yankee Stadium, although home plate is about 20 feet nearer to the stands in order to bring the fans closer to the action.

◈ The Yankees Museum, located on the lower level at Gate 6, displays memorabilia of great Yankee teams and players from the past. The Museum has the best collection of Yankees artifacts this side of Cooperstown. Included are Thurman Munson's locker from the old stadium and a wall of baseballs autographed by former Yankees. The coolest feature is the tribute to Don Larsen's perfect game in the 1956 World Series, complete with statues of Larsen pitching to Yogi Berra. The museum is open from three hours before the game to the eighth inning, and free of charge.

◈ There are about 1,400 TV monitors throughout the stadium. Among them are screens positioned near every seat that doesn't have a full view of the center-field video scoreboard.

◈ The numbering of the sections and seats is exactly the same as in the original Yankee Stadium.

◈ A display board by the gate to the bleachers section features a tribute to catcher Yogi Berra and his "Yogi-isms." He was truly one of a kind!

◈ The 58-by-103-foot center field television screen is six times the size of the video screen at the old Yankee Stadium. It's one of the three or four largest high definition screens in the world and it's really impressive.

◈ Each locker in the Yankees' dressing room has a touch screen computer and safe deposit box. The locker room itself is 2.5 times larger than the one in Old Yankees stadium. It's good to be a Yankee!

◈ During the game, look for Freddy, the rabid fan/unofficial mascot who roams the stands carrying a 'Freddy Sez' sign, a pan and a spoon. He encourages fans to clang his pan with the spoon to help fire-up the Yankees.

◈ Walk around the entire inside of the stadium and catch *The Glory of the Yankees Photo Collection.* There are scores of extraordinary photos that celebrate the franchise's rich history through the camera's lens. These wonderful images of players, managers, Yankees personalities and iconic Yankees moments are scattered throughout the stadium. See if you can guess the players in each photo (they aren't labeled...a mistake). Some are easy (Ruth, Gehrig, Mantle, DiMaggio); others will challenge you a bit.

New York Mets

Park Name: Citi Field
Address: Roosevelt Avenue, Flushing, NY 11368
Capacity: 41,800
Opening Day: April 13, 2009
Dimensions (feet):
Left Field- 335
Center Field- 408
Right Field- 330
Cheapest seat: $11
Most Expensive seat: $460

Stadium Tours: Tours at Citi Field include the clubhouse, field and dugout, press box, suite levels and the Mets Hall of Fame and Museum. You also get to check out the scoreboard control room. Tickets are available for purchase online at the Mets website, by calling 718-507-TIXX or at the Citi Field Advance Ticket Windows. Tours depart from the Jackie Robinson Rotunda. Be sure to arrive at least 15 minutes prior to your scheduled tour time. Cost: $7 for kids, $10 for adults.

Some interesting information about Citi Field:

◈ Talk about some bad planning! The original bullpens had been set up in a way that placed the Mets' bullpen in front of the visiting team's bullpen, completely obstructing their view of the field. The San Diego Padres complained about this unfair advantage during the Mets' first home series after Citi Field opened. The solution: The bullpens were turned 90 degrees, with pitchers throwing toward the field instead of across. This gives both teams the same view of the action.

◈ Be sure to take special notice of the foul poles. Citi Field the only ballpark in the Major Leagues to feature orange foul poles instead of the standard yellow, a tribute to the team colors and a carryover from the Mets' days at Shea Stadium.

◈ Another tradition from Shea Stadium making an appearance in Citi Field is the Home Run Apple. When a Mets player hits a home run, the Home Run Apple lights up and rises from its housing in center field. The new apple is more than four times the size of the previous one, which sits outside the main entrance of Citi Field.

❖ When you walk around the outside of the stadium you can't help but notice an overarching bridge motif in its architecture, as the design pays homage to New York City's 2,027 bridges. The bridge motif is also incorporated in the Mets' team logo. Citi Field is clad in brick, limestone, granite and cast stone, with the brick closely resembling the masonry used at Ebbets Field, former home of the Brooklyn Dodgers, both in color and texture.

❖ You'll be greeted in the front entrance of Citi Field by a rotunda named after baseball legend Jackie Robinson. Engraved into the rotunda's 160-foot diameter floor and etched into the archways are words and larger-than-life images that defined Robinson's nine values: Courage, Excellence, Persistence, Justice, Teamwork, Commitment, Citizenship, Determination and Integrity. Robinson's famous quote: "A life is not important except in the impact it has on other lives," is engraved into the upper ring of the rotunda.

❖ As you take your pre-game tour of Citi Field, don't miss the FanFest area behind the center field scoreboard. It's a family entertainment area that includes a miniature wiffleball field replica of Citi Field, a batting cage, a dunk tank, video game kiosks and other attractions.

❖ Be sure to carve out some time before the game to take a walk through the Mets Hall of Fame and Museum. The museum includes plaques honoring the inductees of the Mets Hall of Fame, the 1969 and 1986 World Series trophies and loads of other items on loan from former Mets players and the National Baseball Hall of Fame. Give yourself 30 minutes. It's free and open when the gates open in game days.

◈ Check out the Pepsi Porch. Located in right field, it seats about 1,200 fans. This seating area, modeled after Tiger Stadium, overhangs the playing field, and may provide you an opportunity to collect an easy home run ball.

◈ If you want to get a flavor of the full Mets experience (figuratively and literally), be sure to pay a visit to The Taste of the City enhanced outfield picnic area. You can grab a bite to eat and mingle with Mets fans.

Boston
Things to do in Boston:

Boston Gliders Segway Adventures: Boston Gliders offers 1 hour, 1/2 day or full day Segway trips around Boston's most popular areas, like the Freedom Trail and the Waterfront. Or you can design your own tour. For example, you can ride along between the Charlestown Navy Yard and the Bunker Hill in the Charlestown area. It's a great way to tour this remarkable city and see the historical icons. For more information: http://www.bostongliders.com

The Freedom Trail: This is a must-see. Be prepared for this to take up the whole day (be sure you have your walking shoes on - it's quite a hike once you add in the wandering around at each location). One note: Reaching the top of the Bunker Hill monument is well worth the effort. The 294 stairs up may seem daunting to some, but the view is killer. It's best to start out in the Commons, get a map from the Information Center and go. There are easy to follow marks on the street and good historic points all along the way. It's free. If you don't feel like walking, see the information above about the Segway tours. For more information: http://www.thefreedomtrail.org

Duck Tours: The "DUCK" is an authentic, renovated World War II amphibious landing vehicle that played a crucial role in the allied invasions in Sicily, the Pacific, and the biggest invasion of all, D-Day. In fact, more than 40% of all over-beach supplies in Normandy were transported by these boats. Your tour begins with a greeting by your Con-DUCKtor, who will narrate your visit, and is part of the attraction. You will see numerous landmarks as you tour the city and then your DUCK goes right into the Charles River for a breathtaking view of the Boston and Cambridge skylines (even though the tour splashes into the water, you will not get wet). The tour lasts approximately 80 minutes. More information: http://bostonducktours.com/

Granary Burying Ground: We don't typically get too excited about city cemeteries, but how often can you visit the graves of the likes of Paul Revere, John Hancock, Samuel Adams and Mother Goose (yes, there really was a Mother Goose)? It's located on Tremont Street along the Freedom Trail.

John F. Kennedy Presidential Museum and Library: Relive the Kennedy era in this dynamic combination museum and library, where your visit starts with a short film and then leaves you on your own to explore a series of fascinating exhibits, including the Kennedy-Nixon debate, the Cuban Missile Crisis, the space program, 1960's campaign paraphernalia and displays about Jacqueline and other Kennedy family members. The striking, I.M. Pei-designed building overlooks the water and the Boston skyline. More information: http://www.jfklibrary.org

Harvard University: I called my mother from campus and said: "Ma, I finally got into Harvard." She would have been impressed were it not for the fact that I was in my 50's when I made the call and was referring to a walk around campus and a visit to Harvard's wonderful bookstore. It may be as close as your kid gets to this esteemed bastion of knowledge, so it's worth the trip. Oh yeah, it's also a beautiful campus. More information: www.harvard.edu

Boston Red Sox

Park Name: Fenway Park
Address: 4 Yawkey Way, Boston, MA 02215
Capacity: 33,871
Opening Day: April 20, 1912
Dimensions (feet):
Left Field- 310
Center Field- 420
Right Field- 302
Cheapest seat: $12 (upper bleachers)
Most Expensive seat: $328(dugout box)
Stadium Tours: All tour tickets are sold on a first-come, first-served basis and are subject to availability. They cost $20 during the season. They last about 50 minutes. The last tour on game days departs three hours before game time. Contact the tour office at 617-226-6666.

Some interesting information about Fenway Park:

◈ The 1st game at Fenway Park on April 20, 1912 was a victory against the New York Highlanders (who would later change their name to the Yankees). This game did not make the headlines in the newspaper due to the sinking of the Titanic a few days earlier.

◈ Fenway is the oldest major league baseball ballpark still in operation. It was built at a cost of $650,000.

◈ When green paint was used to cover advertising on the left field wall in 1947, The Green Monster was created. It stands 37 feet, 2 inches tall.

◈ The red seat in the right field bleachers is the location of the longest hit ball in Fenway history. Ted Williams hit this 502 foot blast off Fred Hutchinson of the Detroit Tigers in 1946. As an aside, this seat is merely a symbol of the home run. The real chair is at the Baseball Hall of Fame, in Cooperstown, NY.

◈ Johnny Pesky hit only 6 home runs at Fenway but one of those home runs was a game winner that just cleared the right field foul pole that is now known as the Pesky Pole.

◈ Former Red Sox players, coaches, or personalities can be found at Autograph Alley on Yawkey Way before games to sign complimentary autographs.

◈ The Red Sox Hall of Fame is located behind the EMC Club near the entrance on State Street Pavilion.

◈ Retired Red Sox uniform numbers are displayed on the right field façade. The original criteria for having one's number retired involved a Red Sox player's requirement of playing with the team for at least 10 seasons and be inducted into the MLB Hall of Fame. However, the team has loosened the rules in recent years as Johnny Pesky isn't in the MLB HOF, yet had his number retired by the team.

◈ For many years, the roof over the grandstand in right featured retired Red Sox uniform numbers in the order in which they were retired: 9, 4, 1, and 8, eerily reminding us of Sept. 4, 1918, the day before the start of the last World Series the Red Sox would win for close to a century. However, the numbers have since been rearranged in numerical order, and now include Carlton Fisk's number 27, Johnny Pesky's number 6 and Jim Rice's number 14.

◈ Check out the left field scoreboard. You'll see the following letters spelled out in Morse code: Tayjry. They are the initials of longtime Red Sox owners Thomas A. Yawkey and Jean R. Yawkey. It's a way of remembering them in perpetuity for those who are savvy enough to know this (or smart enough to have purchased this book!).

◈ The older and shorter of the two John Hancock buildings uses red and blue lights in its beacon to give a local three-hour weather forecast. The following rhyme reveals the code:

> *Steady blue, clear view.*
> *Flashing blue, clouds due.*
> *Steady red, rain ahead.*
> *Flashing red, snow instead.*

◈ Flashing red is also used in the summer to mean the Red Sox game has been rained out. And in October 2004, the tower used flashing blue and red together for the first time, to commemorate the World Series win: *Flashing blue and red, the Curse is dead!*

◈ Fenway Park has one of the last hand-operated score-boards in the Major Leagues in the left-field wall. Green and red lights are used to signal balls, strikes, and outs. Each scoreboard number used to indicate runs and hits measures 16 inches by 16 inches and weighs three pounds. The numbers used for errors, innings, and pitcher's numbers measure 12 inches by 16 inches, and weigh two pounds each. Behind the manual scoreboard in left field is a room where the walls are covered with signatures of Red Sox players that have held court there through the years.

◈ No player has ever hit a home run over the right-field roof at Fenway Park.

◈ In 1940, in an effort to help Ted Williams hit home runs, the Red Sox added the right-field bullpens, known as Williamsburg, which reduced the distance to the fence by 23 feet.

◈ The distance from home plate to The Green Monster is open to much speculation. For years, the sign indicated a distance of 315 feet. Later it was changed to 310, but many experts believe the real number is closer to 305 feet.

◈ The very design of Fenway's outfield walls makes for interesting baseball. Check out the deepest part of the ballpark in right-center field. It's called The Triangle because of the 17 foot center field fence that connects with the bullpen at a bizarre 90 degree angle. Balls hit to that area take completely unpredictable bounces. The net result: Fenway is home of the most triples in baseball almost every year. There are also more errors committed here than in any other ballpark.

West Coast Cities and Stadiums
San Diego
Things to do in San Diego:

USS Midway: The USS Midway is a real aircraft carrier that served in the United States Navy for 47 years. Large and very impressive, it has real jets and airplanes on the flight deck. You can actually walk into and sit in the cockpits of some of these amazing flying machines. Take the audio tour (it's free) as you explore the ship. You should plan on committing about half a day in order to see it all. The flight deck offers a great photo opportunity with your choice of the Downtown San Diego skyline or an F-14 in the background. It's located in downtown San Diego, just a few blocks from the Trolley station, and there is also a parking lot on the pier. For more information: http://www.midway.org

San Diego Zoo: The San Diego Zoo is truly one of America's treasures. This 100-acre zoo is home to over 4,000 rare and endangered animals representing more than 800 species and subspecies, and a prominent botanical collection with more than 700,000 exotic plants. It is located just north of downtown San Diego in picturesque Balboa Park. Leave plenty of time to explore in this fascinating place! Admission is $35 for adults and $26 for kids. For more information: http://www.sandiegozoo.org

SeaWorld: We are Los Angeles-based and have visited SeaWorld many times. You know what? We never tire of Shamu's remarkable show, the hilarious antics of sea lions and otters or the thrilling rides. And how often will you get up-close to beluga whales, polar bears, sharks and penguins? This place is just plain awesome, and while it's not cheap, it's worth the price (about $55 per person). For more information: www.seaworld.com

U.S. Olympic Training Center: Believe it or not, the world of sports actually transcends baseball. In fact, there are those who believe the epitome of athleticism revolves around the Olympics. There is an official U.S. Olympic training facility dedicated to the development of America's current and future Olympic athletes just outside San Diego (in Chula Vista) . You can take a free guided tour of the facilities and actually watch athletes training in nine sports including archery, rowing, canoe/kayak, soccer, softball, field hockey, tennis, track and field, and cycling. It's very cool! For more information: http://www.teamusa.org/content/index/1375

San Diego Padres

Park Name: Petco Park
Address: 100 Park Blvd, San Diego, CA
Capacity: 42,445
Opening Day: April 8, 2004
Dimensions (feet):
Left Field- 334
Center Field- 396
Right Field- 322
Cheapest seat: $5
Most Expensive seat: $63
Stadium Tours: The Padres offer a nice Early Bird Tour for people who want a 60 minute excursion around the park before the game. You can buy tickets inside of 2 weeks from your game. The Early Bird Tour starts an hour before the gates open for evening games (this even includes 3:35pm start times). You must have a game ticket and an Early Bird Ticket to attend the Early Bird Tour. This tour will take you inside the historic Western Metal Supply Company Building (against which the stadium is built), the Press Box, and even includes a cool view of batting practice. Each group is

limited to 25 fans and meets at the VIP Gate near the main box office on Park Boulevard. For more information, call the Tour Hotline at (619) 795-5011 or go to the Padres' website. Cost: $11 for adults and $7 for kids.

Some interesting information about Petco Park:

❖ The trademark feature of this park is the turn of the century Western Metal Supply Company building. Originally scheduled for demolition prior to constructing the stadium, it was renovated and Petco Park was actually built around this fine, old structure. The structure houses the Padres Team Store on the first floor. The second and third floors offer Party Suites. A restaurant on the fourth floor provides terrace dining with superb views of the field. By the way, the left corner of the building actually houses the foul pole.

❖ The designers of Petco wanted to reflect some local flavor into the design. The sandstone and stucco exterior mimic the sandy colored beaches of San Diego. Some of the staircases between the lower and upper decks are designed to look like bunkers, paying homage to the large military bases in the area. The exposed steel is painted white, a tribute to the sailboats in the harbor and the seats are blue in a nod to the nearby ocean. To complete the Southern California look and feel you'll pass a palm court and water walls that lead up to Petco's entrance.

❖ Your eyes won't be deceiving you when you see a grass field directly beyond the center field wall. It's referred to by locals as the "Park at the Park". You can have a picnic or just hang out. There's room for 2,500 fans and tickets are only five bucks.

◈ You sure can't miss the strategically placed 200-foot tall towers that provide support for the lights as well as a number of luxury suites and lounges.

◈ Petco has something called a fractured design in the sense that each seating section has a unique look and feel that creates a collection of seating neighborhoods. And all the seats are angled toward the pitcher's mound to ensure quality views, regardless of location.

◈ As with many newer stadiums, Petco offers the opportunity to purchase and dedicate bricks outside of the concourse Early on, PETA bought a brick and protested PETCO's (the company, not the stadium) treatment of animals and tried to sneak a secret message into the engraving. It said, "Break Open Your Cold Ones! Toast The Padres! Enjoy This Championship Organization!" The first letter of each word spelled out the message, "BOYCOTT PETCO." The Padres decided to leave the brick there, saying not enough people walking by would notice the secret meaning. Until now, that is...

◈ San Diego has become one of the more technology-oriented cities in the world and that theme resonates at Petco Park. There are more than 500 computer-controlled speakers throughout the park that deliver a "distributed signal," eliminating any audio delay from a central bank of speakers. In some sections fans can surf the Internet, check out their favorite players' stats, or order food from their seats.

◈ Every time the Padres hit a home run, a foghorn is sounded. The foghorn is an actual recording of the horn of the Navy's USS Ronald Reagan, an aircraft carrier that sits in the Port of San Diego.

◈ At 396 feet, center field is actually closer to home plate than the power alleys (401 in left, 400 in right), a rarity that makes home runs scarce and low scoring games the norm. This is very unusual because the deepest part of most ballparks in dead center field.

◈ The Padres play host to the local Marine Corps Recruit Depot during games played on Sunday. About 200 Marines attend the game, sitting in donated seats in the upper reserved section of right field. During the middle of the 4th inning of every home game, the Padres salute the Corps by playing the Marines' Hymn. The crowd joins the recruits in standing at attention. It's a wonderful tradition you won't soon forget.

◈ If you like beer, you'll be in the right place. There are 35 different types of beer sold throughout the Petco Park.

Los Angeles/Anaheim
Things to do in Los Angeles and Anaheim:

Disneyland: Welcome to the place where imagination is the destination. For young and old, big and small — it's the happiest place on earth! There is stuff for kids of all ages between Disneyland Park and the contiguous California Adventure. If you've never been here, you will need to spend the day. It's expensive and there will be large crowds. And it'll still be a highlight of your baseball adventure. For more info: http://disneyland.disney.go.com/disneyland/

Griffith Park Observatory: This wonderful building provides by far the best views of Los Angeles, including a perfect shot of the Hollywood sign. Don't hesitate to spend the $7.00 to attend one of the Planetarium shows. There is so much to learn, such as the science behind the seasons, moon phases, tides, eclipses, and recent findings about the sun and planets. For more information, go to: GriffithObs.org

Universal Studios Tour: You get a very cool behind the scenes tour of this legendary studio, which includes the largest movie set in Hollywood history. After the tour, you'll head into the theme park for some very cool rides (don't miss the King Kong 360 3-D experience, it's the largest 3-D experience in the world). After you're finished with the park, spend some time in City Walk, a unique shopping area just outside the gates. For more information: www.universalstudioshollywood.com/

Peterson Automotive Museum: Named for Robert Peterson, publisher of Hot Rod and Motor Trend magazines, the museum houses one of the most important collections of cars in the world. There are over 200 innovative exhibits of cars and motorcycles that will keep any buff busy for an hour or two. Tickets are $10 for adults and $3 for kids. For more information, go to: www.petersen.org

Venice Beach Boardwalk: If you find yourself in LA on the weekend, you won't want to miss the sights and sounds of Venice Beach. It's filled with street performers, live music, skate board demos and break-dance shows. Some would call it a freak show, and they'd be right! There are also restaurants and interesting stores to poke your head into. There are basketball courts and views of Muscle Beach, an outdoor body building club located on the sand. It's a unique place, to say the least. For more information, go to: http://www.laparks.org/venice/enter.htm

Los Angeles Dodgers

Park Name: Dodger Stadium
Address: 1000 Elysian Park Avenue, Los Angeles, CA
Capacity: 56,000
Opening Day: April 10, 1962
Dimensions (feet):
Left Field- 330
Center Field- 395
Right Field- 330
Cheapest seat: $12
Most Expensive seat: $285
Stadium Tours: Tours of Dodger Stadium include a trip down to the field, a visit to the Dodger Dugout, a walk through the Dugout Club (a VIP restaurant and lounge that also houses two World Series trophies), and a visit to the Vin Scully Press Box among other unique perspectives of the ballpark. This walking tour lasts over an hour and is wheelchair accessible. Tours are not offered prior to day games

and begin at 10am and 11:30 am. All tours begin at the Top Deck near the Top of the Park Store and run $15 for adults and $10 for kids. For more information or to buy tickets in advance (highly recommended), visit the Dodgers' website or call 866-DODGERS.

Some interesting information about Dodger Stadium:

◈ When foul poles were installed in 1962, it was discovered that they were positioned completely foul. The foul pole is actually supposed to be in fair territory, which is the reason a ball hitting the foul pole is ruled fair. Major League Baseball made a special ruling and gave dispensation to the Dodgers that would recognize a ball hitting the foul pole as being fair. Home Plate was actually moved the following year to make the foul poles fair.

◈ Between the opening of Wrigley Field in 1914 and Denver's Coors Field in 1995, Dodger Stadium was the only National League ballpark built exclusively for baseball.

◈ If Dodger Stadium looks freshly painted, that's because it is. The entire stadium is painted every off-season to keep the park looking like it did when it opened its doors almost 50 years ago. And that's a good thing, because Dodger Stadium is the third oldest active ballpark in the majors (behind only Fenway and Wrigley).

◈ Dodger Stadium was designed to take advantage of the panoramic views of the tree-lined Elysian hills and a silhouette of the distant San Gabriel Mountains. In fact, if you decide to sit in the upper deck facing south, you'll be treated to one of the finest views of the Los Angeles skyline.

◈ Dodger Stadium was also the home of the Los Angeles Angels between 1962 and 1965. There was no way the Angels were going to refer to the name of their land-lords, so they called the park Chavez Ravine Stadium, the location in which the ballpark sits.

◈ The designers of the Dodger Stadium were very clever in terms of how they terraced the parking lot behind the main stands. Odds are, you'll enter the stadium at roughly the same level at which your car is parked, which makes for less climbing and descending of ramps once inside the park.

◈ Take a look under the Pavilion roof behind the outfield fence. You'll see a bunch of numbers. They represent the retired uniforms of Don Drysdale, Sandy Koufax, Don Sutton, Pee Wee Reese, Jackie Robinson (his number is retired in every stadium but his number was retired by the Dodgers long before MLB decided to honor him in all ballparks), Duke Snider, Tommy Lasorda, Walter Alston, Roy Campanella and Jim Gilliam.

◈ The odds are pretty good that your game at Dodger Stadium won't be rained out. Check this out: Only one game was EVER rained out between the stadium's opening in 1962 and 1976. There wasn't a single rainout between April 21, 1988 and April 11, 1999 - a major league record (for uncovered stadiums) of 856 straight home games without a rainout that stands to this day.

◈ Dodger Stadium is the only current MLB ballpark (exclud-ing the most recently-built parks) that has never changed its capacity. The seated capacity was 56,000 fans the day the park opened and it hasn't changed to this day. This is due to a conditional-use permit that limits its capacity.

In fact, every time the Dodgers add seats somewhere in the stadium, they always remove an equal number in the upper deck or Pavilion to keep the capacity unchanged.

◈ A recent addition to Dodger Stadium is Bleacher Beach. It's located in the upper deck in left field. Fans sitting there can munch on free food throughout the game. However, as you probably know, there is no such thing as a free lunch: A ticket in Bleacher Beach costs about four times more than one in the left field pavilion. So if you sit there, you better bring your appetite.

◈ With the retirement of the original Yankee Stadium and Shea Stadium in 2008, Dodger Stadium claimed the title of being the largest capacity ballpark in the majors.

◈ Check out the distance markers in toward center field. There are two 395 foot signs to the left and right of dead center. However, if a player wants to hit a dinger to center field, it will have to travel at least 400 feet. So don't believe everything you read (except in this book, of course).

◈ One of the reasons Dodger Stadium was built in Chavez Ravine is the proximity to numerous freeways, making for easy access to the stadium in a town like Los Angeles, which is so car-centric. But there is an irony that should not be lost here. When Walter O'Malley moved the team from Brooklyn, he chose to keep the Dodger moniker. However the Dodgers themselves were named for the mass transit streetcars in Brooklyn.

◈ There are more than 3,000 trees located on Dodger Stadium's property. In fact, there is a full time staff of gardeners year round who are responsible for the landscaping.

◈ Look into the hills and you'll see a Think Blue sign. It pays homage to the famous Hollywood sign but puts a Dodgers spin on things.

◈ Dodger Dogs are the best selling hot dogs in the majors. It is estimated that well over 1.6 million are consumed during Dodger games each year.

◈ In a poll conducted by *Sports Illustrated*, 23% of major league baseball players rated the field at Dodger Stadium the best in baseball, more than doubling the votes received by the second place field.

The Los Angeles Angels of Anaheim

Park Name: Angel Stadium
Address: 2000 Gene Autry Way, Anaheim, CA 92806
Capacity: 45,050
Opening Day: April 19, 1966
Dimensions (feet):
Left Field- 330
Center Field- 400
Right Field- 330
Cheapest seat: $16
Most Expensive seat: $200
Stadium Tours: The "behind-the-scenes" tour includes a visit to the following areas: Press Box, Press Conference Room, Clubhouse, and Dugout. Tours take about 1 hour and 15 minutes. Cost: $3 for adults and $2 for children. During the season, tours are held on Tuesdays and Wednesdays at 9:30 a.m., 11 a.m., and 1 p.m. when the team is out of town. Unfortunately, tours are not offered on dates when the Angels have a home game. To make reservations, call Angels Baseball Community Relations at (714) 940-2070.

Some interesting information about Angel Stadium:

◈ The halo located near the top of the 230' tall, 210-ton Big A sign is illuminated following games in which the Angels win (both at home and on the road), which gives rise to the local fans' expression, "Light up the Halo!"

◈ Angels Stadium has been host to numerous musical concerts featuring such acts as The Rolling Stones, The Who, David Bowie, Pink Floyd, Madonna and U2. An urban legend persists that marijuana seeds left on the outfield grass by concert-goers sprouted and had to be destroyed by ground crews. It's also rumored that some still grows out there.

◈ The "Outfield Extravaganza" was created to be the ballpark's signature piece. Built slightly left of center field, the extravaganza is a model of the rocky California coastline and has a running stream of water cascading over artificial rocks. The mountainside scene is complete with real trees and a geyser that erupts 90 feet in the air. Fireworks are shot off from the display when the Angels line-up is announced, when an Angel hits a home run, and after every Angels win.

◈ Before you enter the stadium, be sure to head over to the home plate gate. You'll find a full-sized brick infield complete with regulation pitcher's mound and lighted bases. There are bricks at each field position engraved with the names of Angels' players who played at that position on Opening Day of each season since the Angels joined the American League in 1961. For a fee, the green infield bricks can be engraved with fans' names or personalized messages.

◈ Angel Stadium livens up whenever the Rally Monkey makes an appearance on the stadium's video screens, which can happen whenever the Angels are tied or trailing by three runs or less in the 7th inning or later. "If you make noise, he will come" is spoken over the PA system and soon thereafter a monkey appears jumping around or holding a sign that says "Rally Time!!!" The pre-recorded video features Katie, the white-haired capuchin monkey that played Marcel on *Friends*. The video clip started as a joke on June 6, 2000, but after the Angels rallied that day to beat the Giants, the Rally Monkey became a part of the Anaheim experience, at least when the Angels are trailing.

◈ The Northridge earthquake on January 17, 1994 caused the 17.5 ton Jumbotron to collapse onto the upper deck seats beneath it. Good thing they don't play baseball in the winter!

San Francisco and Oakland
Things to do in The Bay Area:

Alcatraz: This is perhaps the most infamous prison in the country for having housed notorious criminals such as Al Capone. Located in the middle of the San Francisco Bay, Alcatraz was used as a federal maximum security prison from 1934 until 1963, when it was closed due to high costs and security issues. It's open 7 days a week. Be sure to book your ticket in advance (www.alcatrazcruises.com). Alcatraz's most interesting tour is probably the Alcatraz Night Tour, in which tourists are able to take a self-guided walking tour (with the aid of headphones narrating the story of Alcatraz – sometimes by the prisoners themselves who inhabited it) after all of the day visitors leave. Many of the rooms (such as the dining hall) are only faintly lit by moonlight, making the eerie sounds of clinking dinnerware you hear in the headphones particularly creepy. Admission varies by tour, but plan on spending about $30 per person including the boat ride over and back. For more information: http://www.nps. gov/alcatraz/

Chinatown: San Francisco's Chinatown is the largest outside Asia. It's an intense, densely populated area that still retains its ethnic identity. The best way to "do" Chinatown is on a walking tour with a guide who is familiar with the ins and outs of the neighborhood. The back alleys have over a century of history and are still populated by descendants of those who emigrated in the mid-1800's. Yes, it's crowded; no, it's not spotless. This is a living, breathing, exceptionally ethnic neighborhood that flourishes amid the high-rises of downtown San Francisco. For more information: www.sanfranciscochinatown.com

Ride the Cable Cars: Since 1873, cable cars have run up and down this hilly city, though after the 1950s, these cars have been kept in operation more out of historic nostalgia (they are the only moving historical landmarks in the United States). Taking a cable car ride is the ultimate San Francisco experience and you won't want to miss out. It's $5 for a ticket. For more information: http://www.sfcablecar.com/

Fisherman's Wharf Area: This six block stretch along the waterfront is perhaps the most popular destination in San Francisco (we killed two birds with one stone by riding a Cable Car to the Wharf!). There are street performers, shops and restaurants galore (you're going to want to sample the clam chowder in a sourdough bread bowl). It's the ultimate tourist trap, but it's a great time. Be sure to leave room for some Ghirardelli chocolate. For more information: http://www.fishermanswharf.org/

Walk Across the Golden Gate Bridge: You can walk across this engineering marvel as it spans the San Francisco Bay (it's 1.7 miles each way, but you don't have to walk the entire distance to enjoy the experience). You'll get killer views of the city and the ships and sailboats passing 220 feet below. Don't forget your camera, as you'll see the most beautiful views in the world. The bridge is open to pedestrians during daylight hours. For information about parking, starting points and more, go to: http://gocalifornia.about.com/cs/sanfrancisco/a/ggbridge.htm

San Francisco Giants

Park Name: AT&T Park
Address: 24 Willie Mays Plaza, San Francisco, CA
Capacity: 41,059
Opening Day: April 11, 2000

Dimensions (feet):
Left Field- 335
Center Field- 404
Right Field- 301
Cheapest seat: $12
Most Expensive seat: $205
Stadium Tours: AT&T Park has a wonderful selection of tours. The basic behind-the-scenes ballpark tour will take you to places only the players and staffs go including the Field Warning Track, Dugouts, Indoor Batting Cages, Visitors' Clubhouse, Press Box Luxury Suite and more. The 90 minute tours depart from the Giants Dugout Store at AT&T Park. For more information about this and other tours, call 415-972-2400, email toursinfo@attpark.com or head over to the Giant's website. The basic tour will run adults $12.50 and kids $7.50.

Some interesting information about AT&T Park:

◈ The right field foul pole stands 309 feet from home plate. That makes it the shortest in baseball. However, the 24 foot high brick wall eats up more than a few of those homers. The decision to make the wall exactly 24 feet isn't random. It was the uniform number of the most revered Giant of all time, Willie Mays. That said, this may be the only park where players have an opportunity to plop a ball into the water (named McCovey Cove for the Giant's great who would have dropped quite a few into the Pacific had he played in this park). There is a banner touting the number of splash hits – home runs that land in McCovey Cove – hanging in right field. You'll see loads of kayakers gathering in the Cove hoping to grab a ball.

◈ If you're sitting in the upper deck, the first thing you'll notice is the absolutely stunning view of the San Francisco Bay, the East Bay hills and the Bay Bridge. If there is a more dramatic vista in any major sports venue in America, we haven't seen it! Be sure to walk around the entire park before the game and take in the amazing panorama before you!

◈ You'll have a difficult time missing the Coca Cola Fan Lot...just look for the giant Coca-Cola bottle. It weighs 130,000 pounds, rests at an angle of 25 degrees and is 47 feet tall at its highest point. When a Giant player hits a homerun, strobes flash inside the bottle, bubbles appear to float from the bottle's mouth, and green and white lights flash up and down the neon tubes running along its ribs. The bottle is located 465 feet from home plate, and contains viewing platforms and four slides; two 56-foot-long curving slides (the "Guzzler") and two 20-foot-long twisting slides (the "Twist-Off").

◈ Next to the Coca Cola bottle is a 26-foot-high, 32-foot-wide and 12-foot-deep replica of a vintage 1927 four-fingered baseball mitt. It is 36 times the size of the original model and weighs 20,000 pounds. This huge mitt is clearly marked with a "501" sign (the distance from home plate) making it the most distant current outfield measurement sign in all of baseball.

◈ Head over to the Coca-Cola Fan lot and test your arm at the new speed and accuracy pitching machine. You'll get four pitches for $2 to test your speed or for $5 you can test your accuracy by trying to strike out the batter. If you are able to hit the catcher's glove 3 out of 4 times you will take home an authentic Giants jersey.

❖ Check out the Giants Wall of Fame, which recognizes retired players whose records stand highest among their teammates on the basis of longevity and achievements. Those honored have played a minimum of nine seasons for the Giants, or five seasons with at least one All-Star selection as a Giant. Over 40 names appear on the list.

❖ There is a replica of the "Eddie Grant" memorial near an elevator on the left field side of the ballpark. Eddie Grant, a New York Giant, was the only Major League baseball player to be killed in WWI. The original granite monument stood in center field of the Polo Grounds (the Giants home in New York) at the base of the club-house wall.

❖ It's not like they adore Willie Mays in San Francisco, but you can't help but notice the Willie Mays Statue located in front of the ballpark entrance at 24 Willie Mays Plaza. Oh, and it's surrounded by 24 palm trees, in honor of his number 24 uniform.

❖ The ultimate taste treat at AT&T Park are the Garlic Fries. They are served up at numerous concessions stands and are worth every artery clogging calorie.

❖ One possibly unfortunate irony of AT&T Park's field is the Yahoo advertisement at the corner of left center field. The distance to that portion of the wall is 404 feet, which is clearly marked right next to the ad. By sheer coincidence, 404 is also the notorious error code in Internet parlance.

❖ Right-center field features a real San Francisco cable car, with a panel stating "No Dodgers Fans Allowed". Before the first pitch, one fan is selected to ring the bell to signal the beginning of the game.

◈ The fog horn, a feature introduced at Candlestick Park, the Giants' former home, was transferred to AT&T Park and hung underneath the scoreboard. It blows when a Giants player hits a home run.

The Oakland A's

Park Name: The Coliseum
Address: 7000 Coliseum Way, Oakland, CA 94621
Capacity: 34,077
Opening Day: April 17, 1968
Dimensions (feet):
Left Field- 330
Center Field- 400
Right Field- 330
Cheapest seat: $9
Most Expensive seat: $200
Stadium Tours: There are group tours available exclusively on non-game days or when the A's are on the road. Individual tours run $8 per adult and $5 for kids. Reservations are required. Your tour begins on the Plaza between Oakland-Alameda County Coliseum and the Oakland Arena. You will go on the playing field, into the A's dugout and visitor's locker room. You can check out the batting cage, press box and more. For more information and reservations, call (510) 563-2246 or visit the A's website.

Some interesting information about The Coliseum:

◈ Ever wonder where "The Wave" was invented? The first baseball appearance of "The Wave" was sparked by drum-toting, dugout-hopping "Crazy George," in this stadium on October 15, 1981. Many baseball purists wish it had died there.

◈ The Coliseum was designed as a football stadium (it's the home of the Raiders) and was retrofitted to become a baseball stadium as well. This fact is all the more apparent with you look at the backstop, which is basically a notch cut out of the stands. Originally, the backstop was 90 feet away from the plate, but that distance was cut to a more reasonable 60 feet later on.

◈ You can't help but notice the overwhelming size of the foul ball territory. The extra amount of foul territory has been found to reduce batting averages by roughly five to seven points. It's a pitcher's dream and explains, in part, why A's pitchers don't typically fare as well when traded to other teams.

◈ There is no need to drive your car to the Coliseum since it's connected to a local Bay Area Rapid Transit (BART) station. The train station is literally a pitching wedge from the stadium's entrance.

◈ In 2006, the A's closed the third deck of the Coliseum and covered those seats with a tarp. This reduced the capacity for baseball from 48,219 to 34,077.

◈ The Coliseum offers a nice selection of micro-brews. Try a Fat Tire or one of the Pyramid Ales. There's also an Irish pub located behind home plate if you have a hankering for a pint of Guinness.

◈ Junk food tip of the day: When hunger calls at The Coliseum, have a Saag's sausage hot off the grill, topped with peppers and onions, and an order of garlic fries on the side.

◈ Be sure to treat your peanut vendor kindly at this stadium. Actor Tom Hanks sold popcorn and peanuts in the stands at the Oakland Coliseum as a teen.

Seattle
Things to do in Seattle:

The Seattle Museum of Flight: Seattle was for many years the home of Boeing, the world's largest aircraft manufacturer. So it shouldn't be a surprise that the finest assemblage of things related to flight is in this expansive and impressive museum. From the first primitive glider designed by the Wright brothers to the stealthy "Blackbird" capable of Mach 3 and an 80,000 ft ceiling, this museum displays a massive collection of flying machines. It is spread throughout a number of buildings, including the "Red Barn" which was the original manufacturing facility for Boeing. Don't miss the Airpark, across the street, which showcases a number of prototype aircraft such as the first jet propelled "Air Force One" and a Concorde jet. Admission is $14 for adults and $7.50 for kids. You better plan a whole day for this place! For more information: http://museumofflight.org

Pike Place Market: There are only a handful of shopping experiences I've referenced in this guide, but Pike Place Market is an open-air shopping haven that is a Seattle institution. There are hundreds of small merchants offering everything from fresh fish and specialty foods to handmade candles, pens and wine tastings. Be sure to watch the flying fish! If you're a caffeine freak, you'll have an opportunity to visit the original Starbucks location. There are loads of cafes and restaurants in this area. To avoid the crowds, go in the morning when the market first opens. For more information: www.pikeplacemarket.org

Jimi Hendrix Experience: This remarkable museum holds more than 8,000 Jimi Hendrix artifacts in its collection, and is a real tribute to the Seattle guitar legend who transformed rock 'n' roll in the late 1960's. Identifying new ways to experience the Hendrix legacy is a labor of love for this institution created by Microsoft co-founder Paul Allen. Its scope has been expanded to encompass all genres of popular music. After you walk through this museum, you'll give a positive response to Jimi's favorite question: Are you experienced? Admission is $15 per person. For more information: www.experience.org.

Seattle Mariners

Park Name: Safeco Field
Address: 1250 First Avenue South, Seattle, WA 98134
Capacity: 47,116
Opening Day: July 15, 1999 (first game after the All-Star break)
Dimensions (feet):
Left Field- 331
Center Field- 405
Right Field- 327
Cheapest seat: $7
Most Expensive seat: $60
Stadium Tours: Tours are approximately one hour in duration. You'll have a chance to see areas of the ballpark that are not normally open to the public, such as the Press Box, Private Suites, Field, Dugouts and Visitors Clubhouse. Tours depart from the Team Store (open daily) located on the First Avenue South side of Safeco Field. Arrive at least 15 minutes prior to tour departure time. Tours are available at 10:30, 12:30, and 2:30 on days when there are no games. On days when there are games at 6 p.m. or later, only the 10:30 and 12:30 tours will be given. Tours are not given on day games. Cost: $9 for adults and $7 for kids. Tickets are available by phone at (206) 622-HITS.

Some interesting information about Safeco Field:

◈ Safeco's retractable roof is designed to cover but not enclose the ballpark, thus preserving an open-air environment. The structure covers nearly 9 acres, weighs 22 million pounds, and contains enough steel to build a skyscraper 55 stories tall. The roof's length of span when closed is 665 feet. At its highest point when closed, the roof is 215 feet above the field. A push of a button closes or opens the roof in an average of 10-20 minutes (depending on weather conditions). The roof movement is nearly silent, blending in with the ambient noise typically present during a game.

◈ "Welcome to Safeco Field, Seattle" is painted on top of the center section of the roof, visible from aircraft whether the roof is open or closed.

◈ Safeco Field's playing surface is state-of-the-art. It features a specially designed drainage system and a custom blend of four kinds of Kentucky bluegrass and two kinds of perennial ryegrass to provide the optimal playing surface for the athletes, the retractable roof, and the Northwest climate. A spider web of one-inch plastic hose circulates hot water under the grass to bring it out of dormancy in time for Opening Day and compensate for shade and low levels of direct sunlight in certain parts of the field.

◈ Seattle-based Safeco Insurance Company paid $40 million for the naming rights for the ballpark's first 20 years. However, the acquisition of Safeco by Liberty Mutual has opened the distant possibility that the name could be changed before the contract expires in 2019.

◈ Here are some rules that don't seem to apply in open air stadiums: A ball striking the roof or roof truss in foul territory is a foul ball, regardless of where it lands. A ball striking the roof or roof truss is still considered in flight, and the batter is out if the ball is caught by a fielder, regardless of where it struck.

◈ Above the southwest entry gates hangs The Mariners' version of a chandelier: 1,000 whitish, yet translucent bats, swirl in motion. Don't miss it!

◈ The Moose Den, located on the main concourse near the Children's Hospital Playfield, is a meet-and-greet area for the Mariner Moose, the team's mascot. The little guys love the moose.

◈ An analog clock is integrated into the Mariners' compass rose logo above the left field bleachers. Most people miss it…you won't of course, because you've read this book.

◈ Here's something to consider when ordering your tickets to the Mariners' game: Although thick glass plates in the upper deck help insulate fans in the main grandstand, those sitting in the outfield bleachers have no such protection. Even when the roof is closed, the left field bleachers have cover above, but nothing behind them, meaning cold air and wind have free reign. Those sitting in the center field bleachers have a little more protection, as the main ballpark scoreboard runs the length of the section and acts as a buffer against the elements.

◈ You're not going crazy if you think you're hearing trains during the game. There are train tracks that run behind right field. According to Burlington Northern, about five trains pass by Safeco Field during each game, and the trains normally blow two long whistles, followed by a short blast and another long one as they pass by.

◈ Bullpens for both teams are as accessible as any in the Major Leagues. Only a chain-link fence separates fans from relief pitchers warming up. Want to know what it's like to sit in the bullpen or how it feels to face a big league fastball? Just stand behind the fence and find out.

◈ Absent from Safeco Field are any retired numbers – the Mariners are one of only four teams that have yet to retire a number. When they do, it will most likely be the #11 belonging to Edgar Martinez, who played 18 seasons for the Mariners. Martinez remains so revered in Seattle that a street running parallel to the ballpark, S. Atlantic Street, was renamed Edgar Martinez Drive in 2004.

◈ Safeco Field offers a number of exciting areas you won't want to miss. The Bullpen Market located behind left field features interactive games and activities, including the Fan Walk of personalized bricks, local food vendors, an open pit barbecue, and one of the best views of the game from behind the centerfield fence. Lookout Landing, at the end of the left field line on the upper deck, provides incredible views both inside and outside the ballpark. The Outside Corner Picnic Patio, directly above the Home Plate Gate entrance, is a gathering location that provides fans with breathtaking views over Puget Sound, as well as tables and benches for picnic lunches.

◈ There is one more women's bathroom than men's at Safeco Field and we believe this to be the only park that can make that statement!

Phoenix
Things to do in Phoenix:

The Hall of Flame Fire Museum: The Hall of Flame Fire Museum and the National Firefighting Hall of Heroes has almost an acre of fire history exhibits, with over 90 fully restored pieces of fire apparatus on display, dating from as far back as 1725 (think Benjamin Franklin). Kids are welcome to climb aboard a number of the vehicles. Admission is cheap ($6 for adults and $4 for kids). It's a great way to kill a few hours and it's located right in the heart of Phoenix. For more information: http://www.hallofflame.org/

Horseback Riding: If you want to experience the natural beauty of the desert, don't just admire the view from the confinement of your car.... Get out, get on a horse and take a ride with an experienced guide. Explore the "Old West" and its native plant and animal species. With over 40 miles of trails covering 18,500 acres, I'm pretty confident you'll find something you've never seen before. There are all sorts of rides (breakfast, daily trail, dinner, hay wagon and sunset) designed to fit your desires and time requirements. Great for riders of all levels of competency. For more information: http://www.arizona-horses.com/

Deer Valley Rock Art Center: This 47 acre site is the home of over 1500 actual Native American rock etchings. In ancient times, Phoenix was part of a major Native American trade route and these actual artifacts were found along the trail. There's a very cool tour of these amazing pictographs, all of which are between 500 and 5000 years old. Admission is $7 for adults and $4 for kids. This center is managed by Arizona State University, so everything is very real. For more information: http://dvrac.asu.edu/

Arizona Diamondbacks

Park Name: Chase Field
Address: 401 East Jefferson Street, Phoenix, AZ 85004
Capacity: 49,033
Opening Day: March 31, 1998
Dimensions (feet):
Left Field- 330
Center Field- 407
Right Field- 334
Cheapest seat: $8
Most Expensive seat: $150
Stadium Tours: How can you miss the opportunity to tour a stadium with a beer garden, retractable roof and swimming pool? Pre-game tours are available only before Friday and Saturday night games. The tours are Fridays at 3:30pm and Saturdays at 2pm. Tours last approximately 75 minutes and are wheelchair accessible. The cost is $7 for adults and $5 for kids. For more information, call the Tour Hotline at 800-821-7160 or e-mail: ballparktours@dbacks.com.

Some interesting information about Chase Field:

◈ Not many ballparks offer a swimming pool experience while watching the game. However, you'll find one (and a hot tub) just beyond the right field fence. Should you opt for this form of viewership, you better keep your eyes open because the pool sits only 415 feet from home plate and has been the recipient of many home run balls. In case you're interested, you can rent the pool as a suite. It holds 42 people and only costs $5,500 for the game (but that includes the ticket into the park).

◈ The stadium's original name was Bank One Ballpark. However, it was changed to Chase Field after the merger between JP Morgan Chase and Bank One.

◈ Given the rather scorching summer weather in Phoenix, it's no surprise the team opted for a retractable roof. In fact, this was the very first stadium in the world with a retractable roof and natural grass.

◈ Made with nine million pounds of structural steel, the roof is opened and closed with a pair of 200-horsepower motors taking a about four and a half minutes (it does so to music that was specially composed for that purpose). This bad boy incorporates more than four miles of cable strung through a pulley system. It opens from the middle, so the two segments of the roof can be opened or closed either in unison or independently, depending on need.

◈ An advantage of employing a retractable roof is the opportunity to open it during the day and allow the sunlight necessary to grow natural grass. And to ensure ideal playing conditions, the surface consists of Bull's Eye Bermuda, which is considered the most suitable grass for a retractable-roof stadium (but you already knew that!).

◈ The roof is closed three hours before game time, and a massive air conditioning system drops the temperature inside the park 30 degrees by the time the gates open. With over 8,000 tons of air conditioning horsepower behind it, this system is capable of creating enough cool air to chill 2,500 homes.

◈ In a nod to the traditions of the old ballparks, Chase Field features a dirt strip between home plate and the pitcher's mound, one of only two current ballparks to do so (Detroit's Comerica Park is the other). This dirt strip is sometimes known as the "keyhole".

◈ Check out the massive scoreboard screen. It was installed before the 2008 season began, replacing the original one. The new scoreboard is 46 feet high and 136 feet wide and it cost $14 million.

◈ With an elevation of approximately 1,100 feet above sea level, Chase Field is the second-highest ballpark in the major leagues, trailing only Coors Field, in Denver.

◈ Before the game, you'll want to pay a visit to Baxter's Den. Located along the concourse behind center field. You'll find a wonderful collection of baseball memorabilia from each major league team, as well as a historical perspective of the Diamondback franchise.

Southern Cities and Stadiums
Houston
Things to do in Houston:

Johnson Space Center: This is the official visitor's center for NASA, where simulations allow you to experience what it's like to walk in space or land on the moon. Don't even think of missing the NASA control center. There are loads of exhibits, attractions, special presentations and hands-on activities that tell the story of NASA's manned space flight program. This is the only place in the world where visitors can see astronauts train for missions, touch a real moon rock, land a shuttle, and take a behind-the-scenes tour of NASA. Admission is under $20 per person. Even the URL is cool: www.spacecenter.org

Gulf Greyhound Park: I probably won't garner any Father of the Year award nominations from the PC Police for recommending this one, but if you haven't seen a bunch of greyhounds chase a bogus rabbit around a racetrack, you're missing a really fun experience. This is cheap entertainment (admission is a couple of bucks and the size of your wager is up to you). The world's largest greyhound racing complex is air conditioned, has loads of food options and some world-class fast doggies. They generally run at night, but there are matinees on Wednesday, Saturday and Sunday. For more information: http://www.gulfgreyhound.com/

Houston Astros

Park Name: Minute Maid Park
Address: 501 Crawford Street, Houston, TX 77002
Capacity: 40,950
Opening Day: April 7, 2000

Dimensions (feet):

Left Field- 315

Center Field- 435

Right Field- 326

Cheapest seat: $1 for kids and $7 for adults in the outfield deck

Most Expensive seat: $55

Stadium Tours: Tours providing a behind-the-scenes look at Minute Maid Park take you to the Historic Union Station, broadcasting booth and press boxes, Astros' or visitor's dugout and luxury suites. Tours are $9 for adults and $5 for kids. Here's a unique tour option: The Early Bird Tour, where you can take a tour and then watch batting practice from the Diamond Club seats. Early Bird Tours begin one hour prior to doors opening for every evening game. You must have a game ticket to attend. Early Bird Tours are limited to the first 75 fans. These tours will begin in Union Station lobby and cost $12 for adults and $8 for kids. For more information, call the TourLine at (713) 259-TOUR or visit the Astro's website.

Some interesting information about Minute Maid Park:

◈ The design of the ballpark was greatly influenced by the surrounding neighborhood. In fact, the largest entrance to the park is through historic Union Station, and the left-field side of the stadium features a train in homage to the site's history. The 57-foot, 24-ton full-size replica of a 19th-century Wild West steam locomotive runs on an 800-foot track located above left field and moves along a track whenever an Astros player hits a home run, or when the Astros win a game.

◈ Minute Maid Park is the only current ballpark with a hill in center field. Tal's Hill, a 30° grass-covered incline in the deepest part of center field, measures 90 feet at its widest point, and curves around 100 feet of outfield fence. A tribute to Detroit's old stadium, Navin Field, it was named after the man who came up with the idea, Astros' president Tal Smith. Check out the flagpole… believe it or not, it's in play!

◈ A concourse above Tal's Hill features the "Conoco Home Run Porch" in left-center field that is actually over the field of play, and features a classic gasoline pump that displays the total number of Astros home runs hit since the park opened.

◈ For its first two years the ballpark was known as Enron Field before the company filed for what was then the largest and most embarrassing bankruptcy in US history. The team bought the rights for $2.1 million and resold the naming rights to Minute Maid, a division of the Coca Cola Company.

◈ Given the oppressive Houston heat and humidity, the stadium was designed with a retractable roof. It's open about half the time, but don't count on anything but an indoor game if your visit calls for an afternoon game. Measuring 242 feet high, the roof consists of three panels that can open or close quietly in 20 minutes without interrupting the game. Amazingly, the energy cost is about $5 per usage.

◈ Minute Maid Park is known for being particularly hitter-friendly down the lines, especially in left field where it is only 315 ft to the hugely popular Crawford Boxes, though the wall there is 19 feet high. It's probably the most popular spot to be situated during batting practice for those seeking a souvenir ball.

◈ In 2006, the Chick-fil-A cows were unveiled on the foul poles, saying EAT MOR FOWL, and the cows are wearing Astros caps. Anytime an Astros player hits the pole, the fans in attendance get a free chicken sandwich from Chick-fil-A. Believe it or not, it happens from time to time.

◈ Here's a weird bit of trivia. Minute Maid is known for making orange juice. Yet despite their substantial investment in the park's naming rights, Minute Maid orange juice is not available anywhere at the ballpark (although their brand of lemonade is). However, since Minute Maid is a subsidiary of Coca Cola, the soft drink brand available at the park is obvious.

◈ One fun fan feature that has been a staple over the years at Astros games occurs following the 7th inning stretch, when the team pays homage to their roots by playing "Deep in the Heart of Texas." I don't think you're likely to hear that at Fenway Park or Yankee Stadium any time soon!

Dallas
Things to do in Dallas:

The Sixth Floor Museum: Located on the sixth floor of the Dallas County Administration Building (formerly the Texas School Book Depository) at Dealey Plaza, from which Oswald allegedly fired those infamous shots, this historic exhibition chronicles the life, times, assassination and legacy of President John F. Kennedy. The self guided tour includes an audio device (no extra charge) that walks you through the museum. You can sit on the grassy knoll or check out the spot on the street where JFK was actually shot. Talk about giving your kid a leg up on the meaning of JFK's place in history at the location where it all ended. Admission is $13.50 for adults and $12.50 for kids. For more information: www.jfk.org.

Zero Gravity Park: Is baseball a bit too slow for you and your kid? Need an adrenaline rush to kick the old ticker into gear? Here's your place. Zero Gravity is the world's only "Thrill Amusement Park" featuring extreme airborne rides designed to give you the ultimate sense of gravity depravation. You can bungee jump, free fall, get launched into the air, and soar at extreme speeds. For more information: http://www.gojump.com

Museum of the American Railroad: This very cool museum, located off the beaten track, has one of the most comprehensive heavyweight passenger car train collections anywhere. Don't miss the complete pre-World War II passenger train including a Railway Post Office and baggage car, coaches, lounge cars, Pullman sleeping cars and a dining car. You can actually climb aboard and tour a number of the trains. Over thirty pieces of historic railroad equipment including steam, diesel and electric locomotives, cabooses, historic structures, signals and an assortment of small artifacts can be explored. Admission is $5 for adults and $2.50 for kids...if you're really into trains, pop for the $7 ticket that gets you a guided tour. For more information: http://dallasrailwaymuseum.com

The Women's Museum: Yeah, like you're going to take your baseball fan here! Tell you what, if you decide to include this site in your visit to Dallas, just send this book back and we'll give you a refund. If you ever wondered whether your kid has the chops for the complete baseball stadium tour, here is your litmus test: If he insists that a visit to the Women's Museum be part of the trip, take him to an Alan Alda movie and then head home. There's probably a ballgame somewhere on your cable system. Open a beer, kick back on your couch and enjoy the game. You did your best, pal.

Mesquite Championship Rodeo: If you're in Dallas on a Friday or Saturday night (and the Rangers aren't in town), you absolutely have to catch the rodeo. This 52 year old granddaddy takes place in a 5,300 seat, air conditioned arena just east of town. You'll experience big-league bull riding, tie-down roping, steer wrestling, chuck wagon races, bronco riding and barrel racing. This is the real deal, partner...Ticket prices range from $6-$11. For more information: http://www. mesquiterodeo.com

Texas Rangers

Park Name: Rangers Ballpark at Arlington
Address: 1000 Ballpark Way, Arlington, TX 76011
Capacity: 49,170
Opening Day: April 11, 1994
Dimensions (feet):
Left Field- 332

Center Field- 400
Right Field- 325
Cheapest seat: $6
Most Expensive seat: $215
Stadium Tours: Here's a chance to see the club house, batting cages, press box, dugouts and more. Tours are available on game days for night games only. Grab your tickets at the first base box office located on the south side of the ballpark. Tours are approximately one hour in duration and begin at 9am during the week and Saturday and at 11am on Sunday. The last tour is at 4pm. Be sure to get there early to pick up your tour passes as they are available on a first come first served basis. Cost: $5 for kids and $10 for adults. For more tour information, call 817-273-5099.

Some interesting information about Rangers Ballpark at Arlington:

◈ *Greene's Hill* is a sloped section of turf located behind the center field fence. The Hill serves as a batter's eye, providing a contrasting background behind the pitchers which enables hitters to more easily see the baseball after the pitcher's release. "Greene's Hill" was originally designed as a picnic area for fans, but the Rangers have never initiated this policy. The hill was named after former Arlington mayor, Richard Greene, in November 1997.

◈ Outside the park, you can wander up the Nolan Ryan Expressway and stroll along the Rangers Walk of Fame, reading about each team in franchise history on the brick path beneath them.

◈ The Rangers built a retro-style ballpark and chose to honor a number of the Jewel Box stadiums within the design elements. A roofed home run porch in right field is reminiscent of Tiger Stadium, while the white steel frieze that surrounds the upper deck was copied from the pre-1973 Yankee Stadium. The out-of-town score-board (removed in 2009 and replaced with a state-of-the-art video board) was built into the left-field wall—a nod to Fenway, while the numerous nooks and crannies in the outfield fence are a reminder of Ebbets Field. The double deck porch in right field is modeled after the old Tiger Stadium. The park's red brick and granite exterior was copied from Camden Yards and the arched windows reflect the style of the White Sox's former home, Comiskey Park.

◈ The home plate, foul poles, and bleachers were originally at Arlington Stadium.

◈ The Ballpark's 810-foot (250 m)-long facades are made of brick and Texas Sunset Red granite. Bas-relief friezes depict significant scenes from the history of both Texas and baseball. You'll know you're in Texas when you walk around the ballpark and see the cast-stone carvings of longhorn steers on the exterior Texas granite facade.

◈ The playing field is a full 22 feet below street level to help minimize the impact of the strong afternoon and evening Texas winds that come off the plains.

Atlanta
Things to do in Atlanta:

Tour of CNN: Journey into the heart of CNN World-wide and get an up-close look at global news in the making. Inside CNN is a 55-minute guided walking tour with exclusive, behind-the-scenes views of Atlanta's CNN studios and a glimpse of news and broadcasting in action. The tour features history and trivia as well as interactive exhibits that put you in the control room and at the anchor desk of your own television newscast. Admission is $13 for adults and $10 for kids. For more information: http://www.cnn.com/tour/atlanta/atl.tour.home.html

The World of Coca Cola: Atlanta is the world headquarters for Coca Cola. The company has gone all out to create the ultimate statement about their brand. You'll experience a multi-sensory 4-D theater (3-D plus moving seats), a perfectly restored 1880's soda fountain, the world's largest collection of Coke memorabilia, and an opportunity to sample nearly 60 different beverages from around the world. Hey, it's the real thing! Tickets are $15 for adults and $10 for kids. For more information: http://www.worldofcoca-cola.com/

Stone Mountain Park: With more than 3,200 acres of natural beauty, this park offers loads of recreational activities and special events. In addition to finding the world's largest piece of exposed granite rock, you'll have a blast on the man-made adventures. Don't miss the Sky Hike, the largest treetop adventure course in the world. Also see the Skyride, Paddlewheel Riverboat, Antebellum Plantation & Farmyard, The Great Barn, Scenic Railroad, and more. For more information: www.stonemountainpark.com

Martin Luther King Jr. Memorial Site: Start at the Visitor Center and work your way around the three main sites in this historic park: The home in which the leader of the Civil Rights movement in America was born, the church where he preached and the memorial site where he is buried. The complex is beautiful, the staff is wonderful, and the information is powerful. The footage from Dr. King's funeral will probably bring you to tears. The tour is free but has to be reserved and it fills up fast. For more information: www.nps.gov/malu

Atlanta Braves

Park Name: Turner Field
Address: 755 Hank Aaron Drive, Atlanta, GA 30315
Capacity: 50,528
Opening Day: April 4, 1997
Dimensions (feet):
Left Field- 335
Center Field- 401
Right Field- 330
Cheapest seat: $6
Most Expensive seat: $74
Stadium Tours: Guided tours of Turner Field are offered year-round and begin in the Braves Museum & Hall of Fame. You'll tour the Broadcast Booth, a Luxury Suite, the Press Box, Clubhouse and Dugout . Tours start on the top of the hour, and last approximately one hour. Monday - Saturday 9 a.m.-3 p.m. and Sunday 1-3 p.m. No reservations are necessary for individuals or groups of less than 20 people. Tours are not available on days when the Braves have afternoon home games. Walk-up tickets can be purchased on the day of your tour at the Braves ticket window at Turner Field. Cost: $12 for adults and $7 for kids. For more information, call (404) 614-2311 or go to the Braves website.

Some interesting information about Turner Field:

◈ Turner Field was born out of Centennial Olympic Stadium, which was built to host the 1996 Summer Games. After the Olympics were completed, the stadium was repurposed for baseball. Yet there are a few remaining clues throughout of the stadium's past. Check out the curved portion of left field to center field. It's a holdover from the oval shaped Olympic Stadium. And if you walk around the outside perimeter of Turner Field, you'll see the tall posts that surround Monument Grove, a collection of statues highlighting the greatest Braves players in history. These posts were the very columns that supported the Olympic Stadium bleachers.

◈ If you want to stay up to date on every game being played in Major League Baseball, head over to the Hall of Fame. Nearby, there is a video wall filled with monitors airing every game in progress.

◈ Here's a chance to make $1,000,000. No player has ever hit a home run into the third tier of left field. But if a fan catches a ball up there, the Braves will write that fan a check for a cool million. Before you get your hopes too high, you should know that most experts believe it will never happen since the area is 550 feet from home plate and 90 feet high... but stranger things have happened in baseball. Good luck to you (and feel free to split the proceeds with the author).

◈ There's a 100 foot photograph of Hank Aaron's 715th home run in the Grand Entry Plaza. Don't miss it.

◈ Upon arriving at Turner Field, many fans park north of the ballpark, beyond the outfield stands. If you park there, when you walk toward the ballpark, you'll pass over the former site of Atlanta Fulton County Stadium, the Braves prior home (from 1966-1996). The base paths and playing field are marked out in what is now a parking lot.

◈ Here's a very cool feature you'll want to take advantage of: Any time during the game, you can walk the entire lower concourse and never lose site of the action.

◈ If you get a chance, you'll want to pay a visit to the Coca-Cola Sky Field on the upper level concourse above left field. This area features picnic tables, views of the stadium and the city of Atlanta, along with a 38 foot tall Coke bottle. It's actually a great place to have your pre-game meal.

◈ And don't miss Turner Beach. It's located on the right field Lexus Level patio overlooking the field and features a cabana bar, food concessions, a picnic area, and lounge chairs. It certainly makes for a unique baseball viewing experience.

◈ So let's say you're well into your baseball trip and you find yourself burned out on the traditional baseball park meals. The Braves Chop House is an 8,000 square foot dining restaurant located above the Braves bullpen, which allows fans to dine with a better class of food during the game.

◈ The first thing you'll notice at Turner Field is the high-definition video display board. Towering above the batter's backdrop in center field, the massive scoreboard is 71 feet tall by 79 feet wide and features high definition images so vivid that they jump out in a three-dimensional manner. Built by Mitsubishi, this is arguably the most dazzling scoreboard in the Major Leagues. It should be. It came with a $10 million price tag when it made its debut in 2005.

◈ Six retired numbers (including Georgia-born Jackie Robinson) line the façade of Sky Field and the five players from the Braves organization, which includes their years in Boston and Milwaukee, have their picture and number printed on the outfield fence.

◈ If you're a real baseball history nut, walk across the street from Turner Field to the parking lot where you'll find the original section of outfield wall over which Hank Aaron hit his record-breaking 715th home run. Standing in the middle of the parking lot built on the site of Atlanta-Fulton County Stadium, the wall still has the commemorative baseball-shaped marker celebrating Aaron's historic homer on it.

◈ The Braves Museum and Hall of Fame is pretty cool. You'll want to arrive at the ballpark plenty early and take some time to pay it a visit. You'll have a chance to walk through the railroad cars that were used to haul Braves players in the 1940's. You'll also get to see Hank Aaron's 715th home run bat and ball and the knee brace that Sid Bream wore when he slid home to clinch the 1992 National League pennant. Plan to spend about 30 minutes in the museum. It's located beyond left field near aisle 134 and will only set you back $2 per person.

◈ When you order your tickets, keep the following in mind: Avoid the right field "Upper Pavilion" seats – you will suffer as the sun sets directly in your line of sight for the first 90 minutes of a night game.

◈ Turner Field is Hot Dog Heaven. There are twenty different hot dogs offered. Everything from Bison Dogs, Kosher Dogs and the more traditional Chili Cheese Dogs are available for your epicurean delights. Hey, if you don't walk out of Turner Field with some level of indigestion, you just haven't tried hard enough.

Miami
Things to do in Miami:

Miami Seaquarium: The Miami Seaquarium is located right in the middle of the tourist area, on the causeway between downtown Miami and Miami Beach. You'll see dolphins walk on water and killer whales fly through the air. This is a world-class marine-life entertainment park with eight different marine animal shows and wonderful daily presentations. Be sure to budget enough time to spend at least half a day there! Admission is $36 for adults and $27 for kids. For more information: http://www.miamiseaquarium.com

Hit the Beach: If you're in Miami, you have to take advantage of the remarkable beaches. The water is warm, yet refreshing, during the summer months. We stayed in South Beach, which is the quintessential Miami Beach experience. One note: South Beach isn't clothing optional, but topless bathing is permitted. Didn't bother the dads or sons a bit, but when the moms found out, they were less than thrilled. Virginia Key Beach is also terrific and is located near the Seaquarium.

Everglades Airboat Ride: There are a number of companies offering tours of the Everglades, and most are located within a half hour of Miami (some will pick you up at your hotel in Miami or Miami Beach). One operator, Miami Beach 411, offers a tour that includes a visit to Gator Park. You'll see all kinds of wildlife such as alligators, turtles, snakes, fish and exotic birds as you take a 40-minute airboat ride deep into the Everglades National Park. All tours are narrated by professional guides. And here's a cool experience: You can watch someone actually wrestle a large alligator. Fees are $42 for adults and $37 for kids. For more information: http://www.miamibeach411.com/tours/everglades-tour.htm

Miami Marlins

Park Name: Marlins Park
Address: 501 Marlins Way, Miami, FL 33125
Capacity: 37,442
Opening Day: April 4, 2012
Dimensions (feet):
Left Field: 344
Center Field: 418
Right Field: 335
Cheapest seat: $18
Most Expensive seat: $200
Stadium Tours: The Marlins offer ballpark tours, but not on game day (bummer). Tours are available on Monday through Saturday from 10am to 3pm. You get to visit the field, clubhouse (the floor of which is made from reconstituted Nike sneakers), under-the-stadium batting cages and the premium areas/suites. You'll also walk past the world's greatest bobble head display. Tours are $10 per person. For more information, call 1-877-MARLINS or e-mail **tours@marlins.com**. Group tours are also available.

Some interesting information about Marlins Park:

❖ Jeffrey Loria, the Marlins' owner, is a modern art dealer and this stadium reflects his love of contemporary architecture and art. The post-modern, futuristic structure is a major departure from the most recent crop of retro-stadiums. In fact, Loria allegedly drew the first concept on a napkin at a hotel and handed it to the architects at Populous, instructing them "to make a piece of art."

❖ Do not under any circumstances miss the Bobble Head exhibit behind home plate on the Promenade level.

There are 588 bobble heads in this "museum" and each one is constantly shaking thanks to a perpetually shaking display. There are bobble heads from most eras and representatives from all thirty teams. The glass-enclosed display provides a wonderful panorama and the nearby interactive touchscreen enables you to find your favorite players.

◈ Modern art pieces can be found throughout the stadium. It's impossible to miss the controversial 74 foot tall, extremely mirthful Red Grooms' designed home run sculpture beyond center field. It's a masterpiece of bright colors that features moving waves and spinning marlins, seagulls and flamingos when a Marlins player goes yard.

◈ If you walk around the Promenade level you'll catch all sorts of modern art pieces created by noted artists such as Roy Lichtenstein. No other ballpark pays such homage to contemporary design. In fact, Marlins Park almost feels like a modern art gallery where baseball happens to be played. To whit, when home players come to bat, their pictures on the scoreboard are shown in Andy Warhol-like fashion. You sure won't see that anywhere else!

◈ Check out the color of the seats throughout the stadium. There are basically four sets of colors, each tone based on the palette of Spanish surrealist Joan Miro. Oh, and you'll see a single red seat in Section 19 on the 3rd base line. That was the very first seat installed in the stadium.

◈ While the stadium is quite slick and elegant, it houses a lot of steel and concrete. Exactly how much? There are

800 tons of steel and enough concrete to fill a 4 foot sidewalk from Miami to Orlando (about 200 miles).

◈ Marlins Park was built on the former site of the Orange Bowl. This site is honored in two places. In the red area of the Promenade, there is a historical retrospective of Orange Bowl highlights. Outside the stadium, just beyond left field, you'll find the Orange Bowl letters partially sunk into the concrete in, no surprise here, an abstract format.

◈ The three panel retractable roof spans 547 feet on its tracks and has a 216 foot clearance over 2nd base. It takes only 13 minutes to fully open or close.

◈ One of the coolest features at Marlins Park is the half-acre glass wall beyond center field that opens in less than 5 minutes to frame downtown Miami. The windows are 240 feet wide and 60 feet high. This offers the Marlins four climate control options for each game: An open air stadium, roof open and windows closed (to counter the wind), roof closed and windows open (for drizzly days) or roof and windows fully closed for super hot/humid or rainy days.

◈ Enjoy an authentic South Beach experience at the Clevelander. This unique area beyond left field features a pool, full bar, ballpark seats and a total party atmosphere for up to 250 people. Clearly not designed for baseball purists, it's the ultimate party site at the ballpark.

◈ Don't miss the fish tanks behind home plate that serve as a backstop. Each tank holds about 450 gallons. Don't worry about the safety of the fish, as they are protected by bullet-proof glass.

◈ You won't go hungry at Marlins Park. They have thought of everything from the Kosher Korner (Buy me some Knishes and Cracker Jacks…) to Gluten Free food offerings. Don't miss Brother Jimmy's BBQ Pork Sandwich or the Taste of Miami food court in Section 27.

◈ Natural grass is used throughout the playing field, despite the fact that the roof is open an average of only 4 hours per day. To accommodate the shortfall of sunlight, the groundkeepers employ a strain of Bermuda grass called, Celebration, which can thrive under limited sunlight conditions.

◈ The ceremonial first pitch on opening day was hurled by Muhammad Ali.

Tampa
Things to do in Tampa:

Busch Gardens: Have you ever wanted to experience Africa but can't afford the time or airfare? A day at Busch Gardens may provide the ideal compromise. You'll have plenty to do between visiting the exotic animals, riding the roller coasters and going to shows. And don't miss the Edge of Africa section where you'll encounter lions, crocodiles and hyenas. Tigers and water rides can be found in The Congo. You'll want to spend a full day at this wonderful park. It isn't cheap (about $60 per person) but it sure is fun. For more information: http://www.buschgardens.com/bgt2/

Big Cat Rescue: Do you see yourself looking over the vast Serengeti plains, searching for a glimpse of a pride of Lions? Have you ever thought about how great it would be to hike through the rainforest, listening to the tropical birds on the lookout for a Leopard or an Ocelot high in the canopy? Well, this is as close as you're likely to get because this is the largest Big Cat Rescue facility in the world and it's located right in Tampa (about 9 miles from Busch Gardens). A walking tour is $25 per person, and that's a far cry from the cost of traveling to Africa or South America for a similar experience. And your admission price is used to fund the treatment of big cats that suffer the fate of abuse, abandonment or extinction. For more information: http://www.bigcatrescue.org/

Tampa Bay Rays

Park Name: Tropicana Field
Address: One Tropicana Drive, St. Petersburg, FL 33705
Capacity: 45,360
Opening Day: March 31st, 1998
Dimensions (feet):

Left Field- 315
Center Field- 404
Right Field- 322
Cheapest seat: $12 (Party Deck)
Most Expensive seat: $250(Home Plate Club)
Stadium Tours: All tour tickets are sold on a first-come, first-served basis and are subject to availability. They should be reserved at least 48 hours before game day. The tours last about 90 minutes. Cameras are encouraged. The tours cost $9 for adults and $7 for kids. Contact the tour office at 727-825-3162.

Some interesting information about Tropicana Field:

◈ Tropicana Field is the world's only professional sports facility that features live rays. The Rays Tank is located just behind the right center field wall and is one of the largest in the United States. There are over 30 rays that fans can touch and feed throughout the game. And get this: If a player hits a home run into the tank, the ballclub will donate $2,500 to the Florida Aquarium and $2,500 to the player's charity of choice.

◈ Tropicana Field has a number of interactive areas for kids. In the left field area, fans can participate in a baseball-themed game show, take their picture on a Topps baseball card, have their name inscribed onto a Louisville Slugger bat, touch and feel real game-used equipment, and broadcast play-by-play of baseball highlights. Don't miss the Mountain Dew Extreme Zone where you can play stickball in a unique area that has been designed to resemble a New York street alley.

◈ This may not land you Father of the Year awards, but Tropicana Field hosts the only Cigar Bar in the major leagues. The Cuesta Rey Cigar Bar features leather chairs and sofas in which to enjoy your favorite stogie before, during or after the game.

◈ The main entrance of this stadium was designed as a replica of the giant rotunda found at Brooklyn's Ebbets Field, which was built in 1913. Some believe they used the same plans. The rotunda has over 1.8 million color tiles around it.

◈ Only one person who played on the Rays has had his number retired (Wade Boggs, #12). And he only played in Tampa for 2 seasons. Jackie Robinson's #42 is also retired at Tropicana Field, as it is in every ballpark.

◈ The roof at Tropicana Field is just plain too low. The stadium has a non-retractable roof, and although it reaches a peak height of 225 feet over second base, it is only 85 feet over center field (it is slanted at a 6.5 degree angle). Many a player has hit the roof or the catwalk over the years. In fact, the catwalk at the top of the stadium actually robbed a player of a home run. On May 2nd, 1999, Jose Conseco hit a blast onto the catwalk and it never came down. He was awarded a double.

◈ The roof of the dome at Tropicana Field is lit orange after a Rays win at home.

◈ Tropicana Field features the world's second-largest cable-supported domed roof (Georgia Dome is the largest). It's made of six acres of translucent, Teflon-coated fiberglass and it virtually supports itself with 180 miles of cables.

⬦ Tropicana Field's roof drops from 225 feet above second base to 85 feet at the center field wall. The slanted roof reduced the overall construction costs and reduces the amount of air that requires climate control treatment. It is built to withstand wind of up to 115 miles per hour.

⬦ FieldTurf, the artificial surface on the playing field, combines blades of artificial grass with a mixture of sand and ground rubber. The ground rubber is a recycled material made from used NIKE athletic shoes.

⬦ Look for the team mascot. He's a 6'6" seadog named Raymond (what else?).

⬦ When you're at Tropicana Field, you'll hear a lot of cowbells. The inspiration for The Rays' cowbell came from a famous Saturday Night Live sketch involving mocking the cowbell from the song "Don't Fear the Reaper". Since then, it has become a standard feature at home games. Once a year the Rays give away free cowbells, much to the bemusement of the opposing teams. The cowbells are rung most prominently when the opposing batter has two strikes, when the opposing fans try to chant, and when the Rays make a good play.

Mountain City and Stadium
Denver
Things to do in Denver:

Red Rocks Park and Amphitheatre: Now here's something really unique: Go to Red Rocks Park where a drop-dead gorgeous 1 ½ mile trail loops around the red sandstone formations that reach 6,400 feet above sea level. And if you have an open evening, you can experience an acoustically perfect performance by some of the biggest bands in the world. There's even a very cool summer film series that features local bands performing before the running of a classic film. For more information: http://www.redrocksonline.com/.

Coors Brewery Tour: We are well aware of the fact that a brewery tour is typically more adult oriented and it's not something you'd want to share with your kid. However, a visit to the Coors Brewery is actually a kid friendly 35 minute self guided audio tour. This is the largest single brewery on the planet and it's pretty cool to see how they make all this yummy stuff. Best of all, Coors has a tasting room at the end of the tour that serves non-alcoholic Coors-created beverages for the little guys, while you can soak up the real stuff. Participation is on a first-come, first-served basis; no reservations are taken. For more information: http://www.millercoors.com/who-we-are/locations.aspx.

U.S. Mint Tour: Ever wonder where that money for the TARP program is coming from (after it's been taken out of your paycheck)? Some currency is printed and then there are the coins...millions and millions of coins. And if you want to make a point with your kid that money doesn't grow on trees, you need to tour the U.S. Mint in Denver. It originally opened in the mid-1800's to change gold and silver found by miners and prospectors in the surrounding hills into coins and ingots. The self guided tours are 20 minutes, at which time you'll be shown how blank ore becomes treasury coins. You'll need reservations and there are restrictions. For more information: http://www.usmint.gov/mint_tours/index.cfm?flash=yes&action=StartReservation

Colorado Rockies

Park Name: Coors Field
Address: 2001 Blake Street, Denver, CO 80205
Capacity: 50,544
Opening Day: April 26, 1995
Dimensions (feet):
Left Field- 347
Center Field- 415
Right Field- 350
Cheapest seat: $4
Most Expensive seat: $55
Stadium Tours: Coors Field offers a wonderful tour that takes you to the dugout, visitor's clubhouse, press level, club level, suite level and elsewhere in the park. Tours are available every day except Sunday during the season. Tours begin at 10am and noon for evening games and aren't offered for day games. All tours begin at Gate D (20th & Blake Street) and last a bit over an hour. They cost $7 for adults and $6 for kids. You can buy tickets online at the Rockies' website or call (303) ROCKIES.

Some interesting information about Coors Field:

◈ As you look around the park, you'll notice that all the seats are green except for a single row of purple seats in the upper deck of the ballpark. The reason: The elevation of those seats is exactly 5,280 feet, or precisely one mile above sea level.

◈ Odds are you'll see several balls go yard when you attend a Rockies game. It is estimated that a ball hit 400 feet at sea level will travel 440 feet at Coors Field.

◈ If you get lucky, when you take your tour, the guide will point out the room-sized humidor in the bowels of the stadium. But you won't find cigars in there. It turns out the air is more dry than thin at altitude. This was the primary culprit for the excessive amount of home runs hit at Coors Field in its early years. Baseballs stored in drier air are harder and therefore travel farther (think about how far you can hit a golf ball compared to a baseball). Since they installed the humidor, the number of home runs at Coors Field has decreased and is now nearly the same as other parks.

◈ Coors Field has an underground heating system that melts snow quickly and its drainage can suck out five inches of rain in an hour or two.

◈ When you buy your tickets, you may want to consider locating yourselves on the upper deck along the first base and right field side. You see, there's no upper deck in left field, so you'll be rewarded with views of the Rocky Mountains.

◈ The "Rockpile," a 2,300 seat bleacher section, is located behind the centerfield backdrop and offers a unique view of the playing field. Better still, these are the cheapest tickets available ($4).

◈ The Blue Moon Brewery at The Sandlot is a working microbrewery. It's located behind the right field stands, with an entrance from inside the stadium and from Blake Street. It's the only working brewery located inside an MLB stadium. As you would expect, it's operated by Coors, and experiments with craft beers on a small scale. These are perhaps the best beers in the majors!

◈ If you're a concession stand kind of a guy who delights in scoping out everything offered for sale at a ballpark, Coors Field is the perfect place for you. The concession stands in the concourse are laid out so you can walk completely around the stadium and never lose sight of the field.

◈ During the stadium's construction, workers discovered a number of dinosaur fossils throughout the grounds, including a 7-foot long triceratops skull. As a result, when the city bantered about different names, "Jurassic Park" was one of the first under serious consideration. Even though the stadium's naming rights were ultimately sold to Coors Brewing, the team mascot is a dinosaur named "Dinger."

◈ Behind the center field wall is a design that reflects the Rocky Mountain landscape. Check out the waterfall, fountains, and pine trees. After a Rockies home run or win the fountains shoot high into the air.

Chapter 5: Special Thanks and Tools for your Journey

Acknowledgments:

Very special thanks to Kelvin and Ryan Yamashita, who traveled with us for seven years as we journeyed through 2 countries, 19 states, 25,000 miles and 30 stadiums together. Their friendship, shared memories and camaraderie was unparalleled. I can never thank them enough. Frankly, this adventure would never have happened without them.

There were numerous other people who helped us along the way. Each and every one of them did so out of pure kindness. The quality of this journey and the overall experience would have suffered immeasurably without their incredible contributions. I would like to acknowledge a few of these people on the next page. They are listed in no particular order. If I have left anyone out, please accept my sincere apologies and let me know so I can include you in any future editions.

Thanks again. I am eternally grateful for your efforts on our behalf. It really was the adventure of a lifetime!

Folks to Whom We Are Eternally Grateful:

- ◈ David Solomon
- ◈ Howard Heitner
- ◈ Michael Veeck
- ◈ Jim Whims
- ◈ James W. Whims
- ◈ Vern Fuller
- ◈ Lon Morton
- ◈ Bruce Polkes
- ◈ Steve Dings
- ◈ Carmen Molina
- ◈ Scott McGinn
- ◈ Jeff Bille
- ◈ Len Kasper
- ◈ Michael Golieb
- ◈ Al Wolfe
- ◈ Tim Lawler
- ◈ Rich Roper
- ◈ Richard Baron
- ◈ Doug Tymons
- ◈ Rick Binger
- ◈ Joe Vallone
- ◈ Bob Charney
- ◈ Arthur Fredston
- ◈ Randy Gabrielson
- ◈ Jim Cathcart
- ◈ Keith Fisher
- ◈ Joey Glynn
- ◈ Jay Molenar
- ◈ Jerry Silverman
- ◈ Dan Kane
- ◈ Paula Roberts
- ◈ Larry Roberts

Printable Baseball Park Game

Game Date:
Home Team: Away Team:

Home Team:
Boys   Dads

_____   _____

_____   _____

_____   _____

Visiting Team:
Boys   Dads

_____   _____

_____   _____

_____   _____

Alternates:
Boys   Dads

_____   _____

_____   _____

Total Bases:

<u>Boys</u>   **<u>Dads</u>**

Made in the USA
Lexington, KY
12 November 2012